Pagan Portals
The Triple Goddess

An Updated Approach for Working with
the Triple Goddess in Modern Times

Pagan Portals
The Triple Goddess

An Updated Approach for Working with
the Triple Goddess in Modern Times

Rachel Patterson

MOON
BOOKS
Winchester, UK
Washington, USA

JOHN HUNT PUBLISHING

First published by Moon Books, 2021
Moon Books is an imprint of John Hunt Publishing Ltd., No. 3 East Street, Alresford
Hampshire SO24 9EE, UK
office@jhpbooks.net
www.johnhuntpublishing.com
www.moon-books.net

For distributor details and how to order please visit the 'Ordering' section on our website.

Text copyright: Rachel Patterson 2021

ISBN: 978 1 78279 054 9
978 1 78279 055 6 (ebook)
Library of Congress Control Number: 2020949028

A CIP catalogue record for this book is available from the British Library.

Design: Matthew Greenfield

UK: Printed and bound by CPI Group (UK) Ltd, Croydon, CR0 4YY
Printed in North America by CPI GPS partners

We operate a distinctive and ethical publishing philosophy in
all areas of our business, from our global network of authors to
production and worldwide distribution.

Contents

Who am I?

I am a witch ... have been for a very long time. I am also a working wife and mother who has been lucky enough to write and have published a book, or twenty! I love to learn, I love to study and have done so from books, online resources, schools and wonderful mentors over the years and continue to learn every day, but I have learnt the most from getting outside and doing it.

I am High Priestess of the Kitchen Witch Coven and an Elder at the online Kitchen Witch School. My craft is a combination of old religion Witchcraft, Kitchen Witchery, Hedge Witchery and folk magic. My heart is that of a Kitchen Witch. I like to laugh, bake and eat cake.

My website and personal blog: www.rachelpatterson.co.uk
Facebook: www.facebook.com/rachelpattersonbooks
Email: kitchenwitchhearth@yahoo.com

I also have regular blogs on:
Witches & Pagans – www.witchesandpagans.com/pagan-paths–blogs/hedge–witch.html
Patheos Pagan – www.patheos.com/blogs/beneaththeMoon
Moon Books – www.johnhuntpublishing.com/Moon–books/

Kitchen Witch School website and blog: www. kitchenwitchhearth.net
www.facebook.com/kitchenwitchuk

My Books

Kitchen Witchcraft Series
Spells & Charms
Garden Magic
Crystal Magic
The Element of Earth

Pagan Portals
Kitchen Witchcraft
Hoodoo Folk Magic
Moon Magic
Meditation
The Cailleach
Animal Magic
Sun Magic

Other Moon Books
The Art of Ritual
Witchcraft ... into the Wilds
Grimoire of a Kitchen Witch
A Kitchen Witch's World of Magical Foods
A Kitchen Witch's World of Magical Plants & Herbs
Arc of the Goddess (co–written with Tracey Roberts)
Moon Books Gods & Goddesses Colouring Book (Patterson family)
Practically Pagan: An Alternative Guide to Cooking
Beneath the Moon: Witchcraft and Moon Magic for a deeper practice

Llewellyn
Curative Magic

Solarus Publishing
Flower Magic Oracle deck

Introduction

How to work with this book

If you have done any kind of delving into Paganism you will have come across the term 'The Triple Goddess'. It follows the idea that the goddess has three facets: the maiden, the mother and the crone. The triple goddess represents many things such as birth, life, death (and rebirth) and the phases of the moon, waxing, full and waning. Whilst in the form we recognise it may well be a modern idea, I believe it still gives a wonderful way of working with the goddess and her phases, to help us evolve and understand our own pathway through life. This journey can help you to embrace your own personal power.

I have explored some of the myths, history and meaning within this book, presenting you with my own personal views but also information that I have found in my research so that you can come to your own conclusion. My primary focus is for you to find your own pathway and walk a personal journey with the Triple Goddess in a way that suits you. I have hopefully provided you with the beginning of a path for you to follow... Please do read the *'important thoughts'* first and I ask you to keep an open mind.

Important thoughts

In some of the writings and explanations the Goddess appears in three ages, that of the young maiden, the mother and then the elderly but wise crone. I want to put to you the suggestion that they weren't always set in family generations but were in some cases, sisters. Also think about the idea of having a triple goddess but all three being maidens, or all three being crones. And of course, there is the idea of having all three phases within one goddess. I also personally like to include a fourth phase in between mother and crone, that of the matriarch (more details further in the book).

I have laid out details in this book, splitting them into their respective categories because it made the most sense for formatting but please don't let it limit how you see them or work with them. You don't have to look at them as three generations if you don't want to. And whilst I have specified particular attributes to each one there are of course lots of crossovers between them. The crone is considered to be wise but of course the mother and the matriarch bear that wisdom too. The maiden represents new beginnings, but we can all start afresh at any time of our lives.

Also, important to note is that you don't need to use the maiden, mother, crone names. You could create your own. Mother in particular leans towards the idea that every woman must become a mother at some point. Obviously, this is absolute tosh, not everyone wants to be a mother, not everyone can be a mother. This takes a bit of thinking outside the box and moving away from the idea of what the word 'mother' conveys. If it helps to think of her as a creator, nurturer, teacher or something else, do it. Maybe even look at it as being the mother to your own inner child? The idea is to separate the stages of life into bitesize workable chunks. The names are perhaps a little irrelevant. It is the meaning of working with the goddess in different forms and indeed delving into your own spirit and soul that matters. We have become very hung up on labels and putting people and ideas into individual boxes.

See your own reflection in each of the stories the goddess brings, which parts relate to you and your own life story.

And...just in case you were wondering about gender...don't get too hung up on the feminine. Obviously, the Goddess is portrayed as the divine feminine and my personal belief is that she, is a she. I see her as a strong feminine life force. But she also has masculine energies too. I work with her as a strong feminine energy and I balance her with the God for the masculine. But that is my personal choice. I am a proud woman and feel honoured to be a mother. That isn't going to be the case for everyone. You must work with this in a way that you feel comfortable. What if you just looked at these phases as reflections of yourself and your life? You don't have to slot them into male, female or any kind of gender boxes. Working with this energy can help you with all aspects of your life.

There are masculine and feminine energies in all of us. They are the opposing energies, but also balancing and complementary to each other. They are biological, both being needed to procreate but they also exist in spiritual, mental and emotional forms too. Perhaps even more so than physical.

And whilst we are here, let's throw out the idea of ages too. There isn't any set date on a calendar that says 'today I turn into a crone'. Some like to work with the idea that the maiden phase is before the onset of menstruation, once the menses has begun you move into the mother phase and menopause signals the shift into crone. That idea doesn't work for me, but it may do for you. Some girls start their periods very young, shoving a ten year old girl into the 'mother' category seems very wrong. Similarly, a woman moving into the menopause early in her mid-thirties is way too young for the crone phase, in my opinion anyway. It must be your call; you will know when the time is right to move into the next phase of your life. It will be different for each and every unique individual person. Just remember that it doesn't stop you working with any of the goddesses in the other phases. Neither does not having a womb! Don't let boundaries or the ideas of others restrict your journey.

Whilst writing this book I put out a question to a group of Pagans. I posed the question with reference to the titles of Maiden, Mother and Crone. *"The names give us very fixed ideas on female roles. So, my question is, if you were to call the different phases by other names what would you call them?"*

It sparked an interesting discussion. Most people that replied had worked with the Triple Goddess idea and continue to do so. There were some really inventive name suggestions, which I have included within this book (with my thanks to those that contributed).

There were one or two people that reacted strongly to the mother label. The inference being that it doesn't fit in the current times as some women choose to be child free. Whilst I absolutely understand the choice not to have children and I believe it is a person's right to make that

decision, I take my hat off to you (a top hat obviously). However, as a mother myself I am very proud to bear that title, as are many, many other mothers and grandmothers. I don't want to dismiss the mother name because I believe it is important to a huge amount of people, but if it doesn't work for you, then absolutely give that phase another name. Do remember it is just a label, what really matters are the aspects that come with that phase. It isn't all about bearing or raising children. Giving birth doesn't just relate to children, it can mean so many things. You can give birth to ideas, ventures, businesses, projects, designs and creations of all kinds. There is so much more to the mother aspect of the Goddess that can be explored.

A couple of people also put forward that crone wasn't a relevant word these days either, the suggestion being it should be replaced with Wise Woman or Grandmother. Again, I believe that it is the 'bad press' the title Crone has received over the years, even the dictionary describes it as 'an ugly old woman' although they do give a second meaning of 'an old woman with magic powers' which is better. Maybe we need to reclaim it? For me the name crone means wise woman or elder.

Here are some of the suggestions, and I have included them in the relevant sections within this book too.

The Adventurer, The Nurturer, the Wise One.
Youth, Maturity, Old Age

Youth, Experience, Wisdom
Carefree Energetic Years, Productive Fruitful Years, Wise
Independent Times
Dark, Shadow, Light (the dark where you are still learning, shadow
when you start to see both sides and light when things become
clearer).
Act One, Act Two, Act Three
Sister, Creator, Elder
Spring, Summer, Autumn, Winter
Youngling, Mother, Elder
Warrior/Protector, Nurturer, Elder
Student, Teacher, Wise One, Protector
Innocent, Learned, Wise
Youth, Middle Age, Nearing the End
Seed, Seedling, Sapling, Mature
Maiden, Mother, Queen, Crone

And two of my favourites, although I assume, they were said in jest, but you never know!

Knows Nowt, Knows Little, Should Know Better
Student, Quaffing, I aint Dead

If you go along the route of the seasons then you could also work with the elements or compass directions; the maiden being spring, air or east, the mother would be summer, fire or south, the matriarch would become autumn, water or west and then the crone becomes winter, earth or north.

In a lot of Pagan pathways, the goddess is seen as the feminine and represented by the moon. With the god as the masculine and represented by the sun. This design makes sense to me, so it is the basis upon which I work. You may have other ideas, don't let me stop you…make it work for you. And of course, there are examples of the Triple God too…but perhaps that is another book!

Don't be Limited by Labels

The Goddess is for everyone

I believe it is important to note here that anyone can work with or identify with any or all of the phases of the goddess. You don't have to be a teenage girl to work with the maiden goddess. You don't need to be a retired lady of leisure to work with the crone. You don't have to be female or identify as female. You can be any age, any race or any gender to work with any goddess in any phase. She does not judge; she does not discriminate.

Perhaps each of us has all the phases of the goddess and/or the gods within us already. The myths and stories of the triple goddess are there to teach us, support us and guide us. On occasion she may even give us a kick in the butt, rest assured she only does that when it is needed.

The triple goddess represents phases of our own lives but also different aspects of our psyche. Part of our journey is to experience and acknowledge each of these different facets of our personality and even in some cases to unite them. Look to the moon as an example; she goes through each phase in her cycle. She is a shapeshifter taking on different guises as she moves through her monthly cycle. Her phases can also be equated to the triple goddess aspects.

The Triple goddess could also be equated to us as humans having a body, soul and spirit. She can even be seen in the three worlds; The Underworld, the Middle World and the Upper World. Perhaps even time as in the past, present and future. I also like to link them to the seasons, although you need to include the matriarch for that to work, however I have seen the crone associated with both autumn and winter together, leaving the mother as summer and the maiden as spring.

The Hermetic concept of the Three Principles sees salt, sulphur and mercury which could equate to the Triple Goddess.

Salt is the dark, earthly part of the world, sulphur is the light and heaven and mercury is the intermediate.

It's all about the threes

It is important to note that not all goddesses are considered to be part of a threesome (although that has other meanings and who knows what those Romans got up to) and to distinguish between the following terms:

- A *'triad/triadic'* – forming a group of three, a group, union or set of three interrelated people. These three are usually associated with each other or appear together.
- A *'triplicity'* – a group of three identical beings. The quality or state of being triple; threefold character or condition.
- A *'triunity/triune or trinity'* – one being with three individual personas, manifestations or aspects. The fact or state of being three in one. Three in one or one in three.
- A *tripartite* – a being with three body parts where there is usually one, three heads perhaps or three arms. Of triple parts.

Deity - A definition

The definition of the word Deity in the dictionary is:

A god or goddess.
Divine character or nature, especially that of the Supreme Being;
divinity.
The estate or rank of a god: The king attained deity after his death.
A person or thing revered as a god or goddess.
The Deity, God; Supreme Being.

Within the pagan world everyone will probably have a slightly different idea of deity; some think of it as Gods and Goddesses others think of it as one source and every other definition in between, it is somewhat a personal thing. And everyone will visualise the Gods and Goddesses in a very personal way; the God Thor may appear blonde for one person and a red head to another.

Some might see 'traditional' deity – Gods and Goddess of various Pantheons such as Athena, Woden, Aphrodite etc or they may see deity as spirits in all things, spirit of the forest and spirit of the sea for instance. Some may work with deity as energies such as Jack in the Green and the Moon Mother.

You will find your way as you grow on your own path; you may work with all sorts of deities, spirits and energies along the way until you become comfortable with what deity means for you, it will be an interesting journey.

The belief of many deities is called polytheism (the belief in one god is called monotheism). I subscribe to the former, but I also believe in animism, which is that everything has energy; every living thing has an essence. And deity connects them all, bringing everything together. The Earth itself is a living thing, she is female energy and she is called by many names – Earth Goddess, Mother Earth, Gaia – she is the maiden, the mother, the crone she is all aspects, she is all seasons. Everything on our planet lies within Mother Earth but all things are also separate.

Then we have the balance, we have the male energy, the Horned God, the Green Man; he is nature, he is the forest, he is the sun. He lives, he grows, he dies, and he is reborn again. He is the consort to the Goddess.

Then we have the pantheons with all the deities within. Gods and Goddesses of love, war, healing, the sea, the sky, animals, the list goes on. A Pantheon is a group of deities from the same culture. So, deities from ancient Greece would all be collected under the title Greek Pantheon, the deities from ancient Norse mythology would be within the Norse Pantheon and so on. I like to think of a beautifully cut diamond, each facet is an individual, but it makes up part of a whole. I see each Goddess or God as a facet with their own unique personality and character, but also a part of the whole. You don't have to know all the deities in detail, you don't have to work with all the deities, the choice is yours but what I would encourage is exploration. Research, read about, meditate on and investigate all the deities and see what works for you. Personally, I have usually worked with ancient British and Celtic deities because I live in England, I feel a strong connection to them. Occasionally a deity from outside will present themself and I work with them. It always happens for a reason and it is usually very productive and always interesting, so don't limit yourself.

You don't have to work with one pantheon only; some people choose to do so specifically because of their own culture, some because it just happens that way. But as I said before, I don't think you have to limit yourself to one pantheon at all.

At some point along your journey and it might happen quickly, or it could take years, you may find a Patron God and/or Matron Goddess. It might be that a deity makes themselves known to you, or you could read about one and feel an instant bond, a real connection to your core. This deity will become very closely linked with you and work side by side with you, usually for your lifetime. But don't panic if it doesn't happen at first. It took me nine years before I found my Matron goddess or should I say she found me, and even longer before I discovered my Patron god.

Working with deity is so immensely rewarding. We can call upon them to lend energy to our rituals, to our healing work, to spell work; we can ask them for guidance and assistance, for clarity, for comfort, to boost our confidence and to just be with us. Bear in mind when you ask for assistance it might not be exactly what you expected. Each deity is an individual and they all have their own very specific characters and personalities. You may have gotten yourself into a mess and ask a particular Goddess for some help and guidance, hoping for her to be kind and considerate, what you might get is a bit of butt kicking if she thinks that's what you deserve.

I would also add a caution here, I don't want to scare anyone but just need to mention, please be polite, please be considerate, don't summon deity as if they were servants. They are higher beings and they can cause you a whole lot of trouble if you don't show respect. And if you have called upon them to help with something don't forget to thank them. It doesn't have to be a grand gesture, water some plants, feed the birds, put out an offering in the garden (something biodegradable) or if you have an altar set up pop something on that as an offering, a crystal perhaps.

As I have said above, each deity has its own personality and therefore each one has its own specialty if you like, they each deal with particular energies. If you need some help with a healing spell you probably don't want to call a War God. Do some research and call upon the deity that fits the bill, if you are after some guidance in matters of the heart call upon help from a Goddess of Love, the results will be much better.

How you decide upon what deity or pantheon even to work with is up to you, you can do some research and see what resonates with you. You can also do meditations to meet deity. Sometimes deity will find you, you might see the same name popping up when you read things, or on the TV or just into your head...trust and be guided by your intuition as always.

The Triple Goddess - Her History

Where did the idea of the triple goddess come from? The modern belief of them being maiden, mother, crone is usually attributed to Robert Graves. In my research I have found some interesting tidbits from his books and various other 'modern' works by respected Wiccans:

Moonchild, written by Aleister Crowley was published in 1929. This book includes reference to the triple goddess. He describes her as maiden – Artemis/Diana/Isis, Lover – Persephone, and Crone – Hecate. Hecate being the new moon and hell, Diana represents the full moon and the heavens, and Persephone as the half moon, in between heaven and hell.

Gerald Gardner makes a passing mention of a triple goddess in his book The Meaning of Witchcraft (1959) but he doesn't make any reference in his Book of Shadows or his book Witchcraft Today (1954).

Gardner did write an essay entitled 'The Triad of the Goddess' although it isn't dated. In the essay Gardner writes of love, death and rebirth, as a triad and makes a comparison to both the Christian Trinity and the Hindu god's triad of 'Vrahmin, Vishnu and Shiva'.

Raymond Buckland makes a small reference to the triple goddess in his book Buckland's Complete Book of Witchcraft (1986) but not at all in his previous books.

Although his book covers many subjects, Robert Graves does describe the Triple Goddess in his book The White Goddess (1948). Although Graves is often given credit for the maiden, mother, crone idea he also uses other descriptions of trios such as maiden, nymph and hag or mother, bride and layer out. The pattern follows; the mother gives birth to the god of the year, the bride or nymph takes a god as a consort, and his seeds are sown in her womb to create rebirth. The crone or layer out causes some mischief between twin gods, one slaying the other. The death then creates a sacrifice to the goddess, thus beginning the cycle of life once again.

The White Goddess also includes information giving each of the goddesses a male counterpart.

Robert Graves also suggests, the idea of a quintuple goddess, that of birth, initiation, consummation, repose and death as the five stages; these he equates to mother, maiden, bride, crone and slayer. In his book The Golden Fleece (1944) he refers to the Goddess as Maiden, Nymph and Mother, reflecting the phases of the moon – new, full and old.

In Graves book King Jesus (1946), he describes a Great Triple Moon Goddess who represents birth, love, and death. He gives the description as Miriam (Jesus's mother), Mary of Cleopas (Jesus' potential wife) and Mary Magdalene as the form of the Triple Goddess. His book The Greek Myths (1955) also mentions the Triple Goddess.

The 'Cambridge Ritualist' Jane Ellen Harrison depicted the goddess in the form of Maid (Kore) and Mother (Demeter) but combined them together as one. She referenced them to the Christian Trinity, that of Father and Son.

In his 1913 essay 'The Theme of the Three Caskets' Sigmund Freud wrote about the Triple Goddess idea, where he describes them as birth, love and death and equates them to the seasons, the Fates and a tri form Artemis/Hecate.

Eric Neumann (one of Carl Jung's followers) using the quartered circle wrote about four aspects of the goddess. They were Demeter, Isis, Mary or the Good Mother, Mary and Sophia, the Virgin Muse, Kali and Hecate as the Terrible Mother/Old Witch and Astarte, Lilith and Circe as the Young Witch. They reflected birth, inspiration/vision, death and drunkenness/madness.

In her book Spiral Dance, published in 1979, Starhawk uses the idea of maiden, mother, crone as a triple goddess idea.

She also suggests a pentad, a fivefold star which covers birth, initiation, ripening, reflection and death.

The maiden, mother, crone concept appears in Margot Adler's book, Drawing Down the Moon, published in 1979.

Going back further

Take a look at the writings of Porphyry (a Neoplatonist philosopher, 234CE to 305CE) and Maurus Servius Honoratus (a grammarian from 4th C CE) and you will find suggestions of ancient Greco-Roman triple goddesses. Porphyry believed that Hekate has three aspects, those of the new, waxing and full moon phases. He associated her with Demeter and Persephone and also Artemis. He compares the three phases to the three Fates.

Servius wrote that some believed 'Triple Hekate' to be a moon goddess, with Luna above the earth, Diana upon it and Persephone below it. He also talks about the perfect number three and assigns it to God and that the power of the gods is shown in threefold symbols, *"Hekate, whose power is said to be threefold, from which come the three faces of the virgin Diana"*.

Ancient Greece in particular has quite a number of triple goddesses in different forms. If we look at the three Erinyes or Furies. Aeschylus calls them the Daughters of the Night and Sophocles refers to them as the daughters of Darkness and the Earth. They are all crones that reside in the Underworld. Flip forward in history and they were often given separate names. Fast forward even more and they were transformed into the Eumenides. All very ancient but definitely a form of the triple goddess.

The pre-Hellenic people of Attica had three Earth goddesses that formed a triplet. Way back in history, the Arabic people worshiped a trinity of desert goddesses, each a different facet of the one goddess.

Perhaps even the Valkyries are in some part a form of the triple goddess with Hlokk, Goll and Skogul forming a triad. And of course, sticking with Norse mythology we have the Three Norns or the Triple Goddesses of Fate, Urd, Verdandi and Skuld.

Head over to Ireland and we see three goddess protectors, Eriu, Banba and Fotla, triple goddesses perhaps? Ancient Britain has a set of three mother goddesses, although little is known about them, they appear to be a fertility triplet.

The Egyptian pantheon, for instance, is full of triads, groups of three deities making up a family unit however these seem to be more along the lines of a father, mother and child.

There are, indeed, many examples going back through time of goddesses that could be called 'triple' in one form or another. Whether they are different deities or facets of the same one, each could lay claim to the triple goddess title. I explore some of them in more detail further in this book.

And a fourth...

I always feel the need to pop a fourth aspect in between the mother and the crone for various reasons but mainly because there seems to be such a big gap between them that needs to be recognised. I call her the matriarch, but I have also seen her referred to as the Queen. I have included her in this book so that you can explore and decide whether it fits you, or not.

And the rest of the band...

The great Bard himself, Shakespeare, wrote about 'The Seven Ages of Man' as a poem within his play As you Like It. It is an interesting speech made by the character Jacques in the presence of the Duke. You may be familiar with at least the first two lines:

'All the world's a stage
And all the men and women merely players'

It suggests that one man plays lots of different parts, his life being split into seven acts each one representative of his ages.

1. It begins, obviously, with the infant, a baby in arms reliant on someone else to look after them. The role of a baby being basically to eat, sleep, poop and throw up milk.

2. Then a schoolboy going unwillingly to school. But being introduced to discipline, rules and routines. Obviously, Shakespeare's experience of school would have been quite different to modern day schooling, but the principle remains the same.

3. Onwards to the teenager, the beginnings of love (in reality more likely to be lust), the individuality and personal traits showing themselves quite strongly now. Along with all the other issues that fill a teenager's head.

4. Next, we find the youth, Shakespeare refers to a 'soldier' for this phase. This would have included courage, energy and perhaps even rebellion? Reacting to the world around them.

5. Middle age then strikes, when people settle down, perhaps to marriage and families (but not always). Other priorities now take control of life.

6. Into old age. The life expectancy has changed a lot, in Medieval times it would not have been much more than 40, if that, but it has extended. This stage may include retirement now, downsizing, taking up new hobbies and doing things that you might have always wanted to.

7. Shakespeare then adds 'the last scene of all' and talks about extreme old age. The point in life when our body and often our mind, fails us, when we revert to 'a second childhood'.

I think this is quite a fascinating way of looking at life and the phases that we all go through. No titles, no gender specific labels, but phases of life that are all inclusive.

The Triple Goddess Symbol

The triple goddess has her own recognizable symbol, that of the waxing, full and waning moon. But it can also be a representation of the Underworld, Earth and the Divine/Heaven. Or the cycle of life as in life, birth/rebirth and death. It is often used as a symbol of divine feminine as well. The triskele and the Celtic knot designs are also both ancient symbols of three.

The number three

Obviously 'triple' means three and this is a very magical number within most Pagan groups. It has long been a sacred number in many cultures. But why is the number three so special? Our brains like to work with patterns and the lowest number needed to make a pattern is…yup, three. There is a Latin phrase 'omne trium perfectum' which translates as 'everything that comes in threes is perfect'. Even the marketing moguls have cottoned on to three being a good number, apparently when three is used in adverts we are more likely to take notice. The Greek philosopher, Pythagoras was a little bit obsessed with the number three, well he liked triangles for a start! He believed that the number three was lucky and brought good fortune. The number three is seen to represent past, present and future. It covers birth, life and death and the beginning, middle and end. It can be seen as the land, the sea and the sky. Three is a number to represent the divine. You will find the number three features throughout history, myths, songs and stories, even in fairy tales.

In numerology, the number three is all about thinking, intellect and reason. It follows patterns and pathways, making discoveries along the way. Nearly every time you see witches in stories or films they come as a set of three…think about it.

Making a connection

Just as you would with any new person you meet, it takes time to get to know each other and that includes deity. If you find one that intrigues you, or you realise they are trying to get your attention, start with some research. Learn the stories and myths but if you really want to connect, I find it also helps to learn about their country and culture. I also like to immerse myself in the food of the region too. Journey to their home and this obviously doesn't require jumping on a plane and travelling across the globe! With the internet at our fingertips we can travel in a virtual reality to anywhere on the planet. Set up an altar dedicated to the goddess you want to work with, meditate with them. Place things on the altar that are associated with that goddess such as herbs, spices, flowers, crystals etc. Print pictures of their homeland or purchase artwork with images of that goddess and place them on the altar as a point of focus. Invite the goddess to walk with you in your daily life so that you can get to know them before you delve deeper.

Each goddess will usually have several symbols or emblems associated with them. You can create one to help you connect. Get creative and crafty or purchase something ready-made. It could be a pendant, a picture or an object to place on your altar. And whilst we are feeling creative you can work with all sorts of arty outlets to make a connection or express the feelings of the goddess you are work with. Try drawing, writing, poetry, songs, singing, dancing, baking, cooking, sculpting, painting or working with any art form in honour of the goddess.

Once you have done your groundwork, if you really want to connect on a very personal level, then you can work with aspecting, this is similar to drawing down the moon. You invoke the goddess and invite her to enter your conscious. I would only recommend this once you have done your research and walked with the goddess for a while. I also believe it should be done in the form of a ritual to make sure you have protection in place. (I can highly recommend Jane Meredith's book Aspecting the Goddess for more details on this).

The Triple Goddesses

Included here, is a little information about some of the suggested triple goddess groups. I have looked at academic and historical information, rather than spiritual, to get the 'facts' as much as possible. You may prefer to see them from a more spiritual angle. Are they all definitely triple goddesses? I think very few of them are, some triads, some trios, some just groups. Very few of them fit the exact description of a triple goddess, but I present to you the basics and you can do your own further research and make a decision for yourself.

Aglaia, Euphrosyne, Thalia

These three lovelies were sisters, all daughters of Zeus, the Greek King of the Gods and Eurynome, an Oceanid, water nymph. Although some stories suggest their mother was Hera. Other stories quote their parents as Helios and Aegle. They are known as the Three Graces, Charities or Kharites. Collectively they represent grace, charm and beauty, although they have their own individual qualities too.

Aglaia – elegance, magnificence, adornment, brightness and splendour. She was also named Kharis (Grace) and Kale (Beauty). Aglaia was wife to the god Hephaistos and mother to four younger Kharites.

Euphrosyne – mirth, joy, cheerfulness, merriment (bit of a good time gal this one). Her name derives from the Greek word 'euphrosynos' which means merriment.

Thalia – youth, beauty, cheerfulness, festivity, richness, luxury and banquets. Her name derives from the Greek word 'thalia' a term that means abundant and luxurious banquets. It also means 'the blooming' which could relate to springtime.

Basically, their job was to spread beauty and charm to all young women, and to share general feelings of joy and goodwill amongst all people. They were often attendants to Venus, Apollo, Aphrodite and Hera and on a first name basis with The Muses. Although Thalia could be classed as a maiden, the other sisters don't fit into the stereotype triple goddess role of mother and crone.

Al-Uzza, Al-Lat, Manat/Manawayat

A triad of goddesses from pre-Islamic Arabia. Sometimes all referred to as the daughters of Al-Lah (the God) and Manat and Al-Lat are occasionally seen as daughters of Al-Uzza.

Al-Uzza – her name translates as 'the mighty one', she is the Goddess of the morning and evening star. A 5th Century CE writer, Isaac of Antioch, wrote that women would stand on their rooftops and invoke this goddess. In the 4th Century CE, St Epiphanius used a title 'Chaamu' for her, which translates as 'young girl' or 'virgin'. She is a strong goddess who covers both love and war.

Al-Lat – her name translates as 'the Goddess', she is seen as the mother. In ancient writings she has been referred to as 'Mother of the Gods' and 'Greatest of All'. As an Earth goddess she covers spring, fertility and prosperity. In Arabia the sun was considered to be a feminine energy and could have been associated with her. Images of her can be seen with a crescent moon and also a sun disk.

Manat – which means fate, time or destruction, she is often depicted as the crone. She has connection to a sanctuary that was the point where people set off on pilgrimages. Worship of her is very ancient and may precede Al-Lat and Al-Uzza. She is a goddess of death and would protect tombs from those wishing to desecrate them. Seemingly a triple goddess set in the form of maiden, mother, crone.

Aphrodite, Hera, Athena

These three Greek goddesses are often included in lists of

triple goddesses, although I believe it is purely down to their appearance in the Greek myth 'The Judgement of Paris'. Nothing else particularly links them as a group. However, this is a brief summary of the story so you can judge for yourself.

This myth is the story of a beauty pageant. It begins with a wedding, that of Peleus and Thetis. Everyone that was anyone was invited, except for Eris, the goddess of discord (which is not a surprise, who wants discord at a wedding?) Anyway, she rocks up to the wedding and gets turned away at the door. This makes her angry and she throws a golden apple into the group of goddesses with the label 'to the fairest'. It was a challenge. Three of the goddesses stepped forward, Aphrodite, Hera and Athena. Zeus took charge as the mediator and asked the god Hermes to take the goddesses to Paris of Troy (a mortal prince, son of King Priam). Each goddess appeared before the Prince, each one offering him bribes to pick them. Hera promised wealth and a high position of authority and Athena offered skill, knowledge and warrior powers. His choice though was Aphrodite, she promised him Helen as a bride. Sadly, it went horribly wrong, Helen was abducted which was followed by the Trojan War and the subsequent fall of the city.

Arthur's Queens

One of the most famous stories is of King Arthur and his Knights of the round table, along with the sorcerer Merlin. In this we see three great Queens in the form of Guenievere: Gwenhwyfar, daughter of Cywryd Gwent, and Gwenhwyfar daughter of Gwythyr ap Greidol son of Greidiawl, and Gwenhwyfar daughter of Gogfran/Ogrfan Gawr the Giant (did you make sense of all that?). Welsh Triads claim that Arthur was married three times, to these ladies all named Guinevere (well that's a bit convenient). Some stories present them as daughters of the gods of death and light. It might be due to confusion over her parentage or perhaps a triple goddess aspect?

Artemis, Selene, Hecate

It seems that we have Roman poets to thank for this triad of Greek goddesses. Quite a few of them mention them as a triad. Nonnus wrote in 5thC CE describing Selene, Hekate and Artemis in a triple goddess scene. Statius in the 1st C CE describes a triple goddess with these three deities. Seneca writes about them as a triad in several cases circa 1st C CE. For me it seems that these three have been grouped together but I am not certain they really form a triple goddess set, although they could be worked to fit the maiden, mother, crone roles if you chose to.

Blodeuwedd, Arianrhod, Cerridwen

Although Cerridwen embodies all three aspects of the triple goddess within herself. She is often seen in the company of her fellow Welsh goddesses, Blodeuwedd as the maiden, Arianrhod as the mother and Cerridwen takes the role of crone.

Blodeuwedd – is known as the flower face goddess, because that's how she was created, from flowers. In this set she is the maiden, a goddess of spring, beauty (albeit temporary), death and omens.

Arianrhod – plays the part of the mother in this triplet. She is a goddess of fertility, rebirth, the moon and time. She helps lead those that have departed, to the Otherworld.

Cerridwen – is a goddess of inspiration, wisdom, transformation and rebirth. She is the keeper of the cauldron, having brewed the Awen, or potion of wisdom, inspiration and knowledge. Seen as the crone aspect in this particular triple goddess set, although for me she is much more, encompassing all of the different phases herself. I usually 'see' her as a mother figure to be honest. If you are looking for a triple goddess gang, then this is probably one of the most recognisable modern versions.

Brigit/Brighid

If you take a look in Cormac's Glossary it tells of three Brigits, all of them sisters each with a different skill. A poet, a smith and a healer. But they aren't maiden, mother, crone in fact they are seen as similar or the same in age. There are a lot of stories about Brigit, she is ancient and found across Ireland, Scotland, Wales, Britain and Gaul. It does seem quite difficult to separate each facet in the stories. The general view is her father was Dagda, descriptions title her as 'daughter or daughters of Dagda'. She is married to Eochaid Bres and had a son called Ruadan. Although there are also tales of her bearing three sons, those sons being called Brian, Iachar and Iucharba. Brighid is also the sister to Angus MacOg. Later on, she was renamed as a Saint and thought to be the foster mother of Christ, this gives her the role of mother. She was also given the image of being a mother of the Gods. As a group of three she is the three daughters of the Dagda, each with their own skills and abilities. She is also seen in another trio, as Brigid the Hospitaller, Brigid the Judgments and Brigid of the Cowless. The first is mother of Senchan, Judge of the Ulster court, the second is his wife and the latter his daughter. As the mother she provides hospitality and comfort, as the wife she dishes out judgements and as the daughter she is a young unmarried warrior/hunter.

Most myths and tales speak of a single goddess so it might be difficult to decide which Brighid is which in the stories, I will leave it up to you to research and discover all the aspects.

The Camenae: Antevorta, Carmenta, Postvorta and Aegeria

Let me introduce you to a group of water nymphs from ancient Rome who had the skills of prophecy and poetry and were also known as birth goddesses. They look after springs and water and were called upon primarily for healing. Camenae comes from the Latin word 'carmen' which means 'charm, song, poem, prayer or magical formula'. They presided in a sacred grove with a fountain on Caelian Hill in Rome. The spring was famous for its healing and health-giving waters. The water was carried daily to the Temple of Vesta and consecrated to the Vestal Virgins. Often seen as three, they were sometimes a group of four. The leader was Carmenta who in some stories was said to have come originally from Greece. She lived to be 110 years old, I assume she must have taken plenty of the healing waters herself! She had legendary divination skills but also protected mothers and children during childbirth.

Antevorta and Postvorta may have initially been different aspects of Carmenta, but became individuals in their own right eventually, albeit in the form of sisters or even attendants of Carmenta. The name Antevorta translates as 'before change' and Postvorta 'after change'.

Aegeria appears to be quite an important member of the team, and she appears as a goddess of springs and prophecy, however she doesn't seem to be related to Carmenta. The Romans as some point renamed the Muses as the Camenae.

Corn Woman: Corn Maiden, Corn Mother, Yellow Woman

Here we have the Corn Woman, a figure from the indigenous tribes of North America. As with a lot of myths, there are several versions.

The Corn Mother is seen as an old woman who manages to feed her tribe by rubbing her body, as she does so it produces grains of corn. However, one of the tribe discovers how she is providing the corn, they are unimpressed, she is accused of witchcraft and killed. But the ground where her body is buried continues to produce corn. Her attributes are harvest, abundance, fertility and health. She is also associated with children.

Another version tells of a Corn Maiden, a young and beautiful woman who marries into a tribe. She produces corn to feed them. When the tribe discovers how the corn is made, they are revolted. She runs from the tribe and returns to her original home. Her husband seeks her, and she gives him some corn along with instructions on how to grow it properly.

There are also stories that tell of 'Corn Maidens' in the plural. Each maiden bringing one seed of corn to be nurtured and grown to help the tribe. Corn Maiden also seems to be referred to as 'grandmother of sun and light', which conflicts with our general idea of a maiden.

Yellow Woman appears in stories often with her sisters, blue, white and red corn. Her stories seem to be for the most part about how she is alienated from everyone, living on the edge of the village or refusing to marry. She appears to be the spirit of womanhood.

There are many and varied versions throughout this culture, all featuring corn in various ways and keeping the tribe fed and alive. Are these seen as a triple goddess? I am inclined to say no. I think the Corn Maiden and Corn Mother in particular are one and the same. But I don't know enough about the indigenous peoples of North America to make that call.

Diana Trivia

Diana Trivia is a Roman goddess. The word trivia comes from the Latin 'trivium' which translates as 'crossroads', so she is goddess of the crossroads, particularly when that crossroads is made from three roads. She represents three aspects, that of the huntress, the moon and the Queen of the Underworld. Seneca's Medea (a Roman tragedy from the first century) refers to the Trivia, in the form of the triple goddess Hecate, Selene and Diana. Diana being the maiden and the huntress, Selene being the mother in the form of the full moon and Hecate as the crone. Perhaps one of the closest ideals of a triple goddess.

Eriu, Banba and Fotla

These ladies are sisters, along with Badb, Macha, Banba and the Morrigan, who represent the sovereignty of Ireland. However, some stories tell they were not sisters to Badb, Macha and the Morrigan, but worshipped them. They are daughters of the Ernmas. Three names for Ireland, each of them married to a King of Ireland, the brothers Mac Cuill, Mac Cecht and Mac Greinne. Their husbands are all grandsons of the Dagda and interestingly triplets. Although there are suggestions that the parentage is not accurate.

The name Eriu could well be translated from the Celtic word meaning 'land'. The name Banba translates as 'place of women's death'. The name Fotla could mean 'grassy land'. A triple goddess perhaps, but they are a trio of goddesses, each one of them a representation of the land of Ireland.

Erinyes/Furies/Eumenides; Tisiphone, Alecto, Megaera

Here we have three Greek goddesses of vengeance and retribution, although, to be fair, they focused on punishing men for crimes against the natural order rather than just throwing vengeance about carefree. They were apparently not a pretty sight; beauty was not on the agenda and they sported wings. Their hair and bodies were covered with poisonous snakes. Oh, and they also carried whips. Most images seem to portray them all as maidens.

If you felt you were the victim you could call upon the Erinyes to dish out some justice. I assume it was a good deterrent, as the punishment given out could include madness, disease, hunger or even death. If you wanted to seek their forgiveness (assuming you weren't already dead) you could complete a ritual and a specific task that was set for you. The Erinyes also served Hades and Persephone in the Underworld.

Their names appeared in later writings. Alecto was 'unceasing in anger', Tisiphone 'avenger of murder' and Megaera 'jealousy'.

People feared to even mention the name Erinyes, so they were often referred to by other names such as Eumenides.

There is also a play, a trilogy in fact, written by the ancient Greek playwright Aeschylus. The play was performed at the annual Dionysia festival in Athens in 458 BCE. It won first prize. The trilogy was titled The Oresteia, the third of the linked tragedies was called The Eumenides. It features of course, the Erinyes. Not triple goddesses as we recognize that they were all maidens, but a formidable trio of goddesses.

The Three Fates/Moirai/Moirae

Three ancient Greek goddesses of fate. The name translates as 'parts/shares or portions.' Individually they are Klotho (Clotho), she is the spinner, spinning out the thread of life. Lakhesis (Lachesis), the 'apportioner of lots' she measures it all and Atropos (Asia) 'she who cannot be turned' who cuts it down short. They were led by the god of fate, Zeus Moiragetes.

When a human is born, the Fates spin out the thread that builds their future. It isn't a future set in stone, if Zeus wants to step in and redirect that fate he does. Obviously, humans themselves also have a hand in their own fates too. But these three had powers, they could direct and divert the fate of any man. They worked alongside the Erinyes. Their appearance was not pretty. Said to be old, ugly women. Klotho carries a spindle, Lakhesis a staff and Atropos a scroll or scales. The Romans called them the Parcae and their names were Nona, Decuma and Morta. A Triple Goddess? Definitely three individuals but part of a group and all crones.

Gorgons/Gorgones

Greek winged daimones who came in a set of three. Probably one of the most recognized is Medusa/Medousa, with her two sisters Sthenno and Euryale. Some poets described Medusa as a beautiful woman who angered Athena by sleeping with

Poseidon, her punishment was to be turned into a gorgon. Other stories just give her as always being a gorgon. Medusa was mortal, although her two sisters were not. This left her slightly vulnerable, despite her obvious skill of turning men to stone with one glance. Perseus was the one to do the dirty deed. He chopped off her head, aided by a reflective shield, winged boots and a very large sword, oh and the ability to become invisible. When her head was severed from her body, the surprise was Pegasus, the winged horse and Khrysaor the giant both emerged from the wound.

Greek artwork shows the three gorgons with wings and snakes for hair, they also sported tusks and occasionally beards – sounds attractive...A triple goddess? Perhaps, or just a set of three sisters?

Harpies

This term is used in modern language to describe a particular type of woman, not a pleasant one. However, the Harpies (Harpyiai) stem from ancient Greece. They are wind demons/ daimones/spirits. Zeus would send his harpies out to remove people or objects from earth, in sudden swift movements. Anyone that disappeared suddenly or mysteriously was said to have been taken by the Harpies. Images show them as ugly winged half woman, half bird. Triple goddess? Just a group of demons, I think.

Hathor, Sekhmet, Bast

Seen with a lion head, Sekhmet is one of the most ancient of Egyptian goddesses. Her name translates as 'powerful one'. She has a bit of a reputation as being the harder aspect of the more fun, fertile and happy goddess Hathor. They share a temple built by Amenemhet II dedicated to them both. One of Sekhmet's names was 'the destroyer' so you can see where we are going with this. She is the power of the hot midday sun and was seen as a pretty scary deity. Although she was the patron of healers, so she also brought life and healing. A creator and destroyer. Oh, and she could send plagues if someone upset her.

Hathor was created by the god Ra, who plucked her from Ureas' brow and sent her to earth as a lion. She was there to punish mankind for not obeying his laws. She caused quite a stir, actually, it was described as a blood bath. To stop her, Ra poured 7000 jugs of beer and pomegranate juice in front of her, she drunk it all and slept for three days. On awakening she felt much better and the blood lust stopped. See... it only took 7000 pints of beer! Hathor is a goddess of song, fertility, happiness and pretty much all good things. She is a goddess of the stars and the heavens.

Bast features in some legends as a twin or counterpart to Sekhmet. Sekhmet from Upper Egypt and Bast from Lower Egypt. And then Hathor represents Upper Egypt as well. Originally a lion-headed goddess she soon became associated more with the cat. Originally believed to be the daughter of Atum, she is now thought to be another daughter of Ra. Her name is also associated with the blood lust/beer story with her being the 'eye of Ra' rather than Hathor. She is also linked with Sekhmet as they both have lion heads but also seemingly both married to Ptah.

Are they a triple goddess? Some like to suggest that Bast is the maiden, Hathor the mother and Sekhmet the crone. It is an interesting idea. Hathor and Sekhmet do seem to have a definite connection, being aspects of the same goddess, how ancient that connection is, however, I am not sure. Does Bast fit into the trio? Possibly not.

Hathor, Nephthys, Isis

Ancient Egyptian goddesses Isis and Hathor, it seems are very much alike, often in images they are identical. It also seems that Isis upset Horus, who then chopped off her head – in its place she grew the head of a cow, which is the form Hathor is most often seen in. Isis is also a sister to Nephthys, again both are very similar in appearance. The sisters were protectors of the living and the dead.

A triple goddess? I think perhaps they have a link, as so many images of them seem to be similar if not identical, I am not sure that makes them a triple goddess though.

Hekate/Hecate

A Greek goddess of magic and witchcraft. She helped the goddess Demeter when she was looking for her daughter Persephone, guiding her with flaming torches. She is a goddess of the crossroads. Her name translates as 'worker from afar'. She is often associated with other goddesses, but I think her tripleness (is that a word?) comes from within her. She bears many titles, some of which are Dark Maiden, Dark Mother and Dark Queen to name only a few. Each sees her in different guises or stages of life. Sometimes she is seen as an individual deity, others as a triple form. Ancient artwork shows her as a beautiful young nymph, however more modern versions see her as a crone. As a triple form she is depicted with three heads, those of animals. A triple goddess? Not in the separate form but I do think she perhaps holds the idea well, but all within the one goddess. She is definitely a formidable deity to deal with.

Hesperides

Three Greek nymphs who embodied the evening and sunsets. Daughters of the goddess of the night, Nyx, they took care of the golden apple tree that belonged to Hera. Ably assisted by a hundred headed dragon (I definitely need to get one of those). They also looked after other bounty that belonged to the gods. Triple goddess? No, I guess not, but an interesting trio of goddesses.

The Horae

The Horae is a name that covers two separate groups of Greek goddesses. One set covers the twelve hours during the day. Sisters to the Moirae (Fates), the set we are looking at is three goddesses that deal with the seasons and the time set by nature. Their names are Eunomia meaning good order or good pasture, Eirene translating as peace or spring and Dike which means justice. They were worshipped by farmers in particular to help with the growth and success of crops. They meet some of the criteria for a triple goddess set, I think.

Inanna, Ishtar, Astarte

Often referred to as Lady of the Heavens this title has been bestowed on several different deities. In Sumeria she was Inanna, in the Akkadian Empire she was Ishtar and the Canaanite people knew her as Astarte. Ishtar's following is an ancient one and she has taken on the role of a sex, war, love and fertility goddess and also deals with the morning and evening star – she is one busy woman. Her images mostly show her as quite a sexy winged lady. She also covers the seasons of spring and summer. She has a dual role as both mother and wife to Tammuz. At some point Inanna become Ishtar, a name that originates from Attar/Ashtart. Seemingly at this point she also gained the addition of male attributes. Astarte is perhaps a little separate from Inanna and Ishtar, but it does seem Ishtar was an influence on Astarte, she certainly seems to have very similar characteristics. A Triple Goddess? I think not.

Kore/Persephone, Demeter, Hekate

Persephone is a goddess of spring and vegetation; her mother is Demeter a goddess of agriculture and harvest and then we have Hekate (see her details above). The story begins with Persephone being kidnapped by Hades, King of the Underworld who forces her to marry him, thus, making her a goddess of the

Underworld. Demeter, her mother, desperately looks for her and with the help of Hekate she rescues her. However, Hades feeds Persephone pomegranate seeds, this binds her to him so that she must come into the Underworld for half the year. Here we have an explanation for the seasons, Persephone being in the Underworld for half the year causes the winter, when she emerges, she brings the spring and the summer. Obviously, that's the short version of the story.

Persephone could be seen as the maiden, with Demeter as the mother. The issue is with Hekate, although in modern times she is often depicted as a crone, which would work with the Triple Goddess idea. In some stories Persephone is not named as such until she is married, before that she is called Kore. If you work with Kore as the maiden and then Demeter as the mother followed by the transformed Persephone as the crone, you get a triple goddess. The name Kore translates as 'the maiden' and then Demeter is 'earth mother' with the meaning of Persephone being 'destroyer of light'. I am not convinced by either, but it may work for you.

Proserpina, Ceres

And to mirror the Greek Persephone tale we have the Roman version which is pretty much the same story. Persephone is Proserpina and Demeter is Ceres. In the Roman story, Proserpina is kidnapped by Pluto instead of Hades. Although there doesn't appear to be a crone goddess in this story. The negotiation for rescue comes from the god, Jupiter, sent via Mercury to release Proserpina. Proserpina definitely embodies all the maiden characteristics as Ceres does for the mother phase.

The Matronae

The challenge with this little group is the lack of evidence. There are a few mentions of them across Europe, inscriptions on plaques, altars and statues. They are referred to as Matronae,

Matres or Nutrices. But there doesn't seem to be any actual stories or myths. They were revered throughout the Roman Empire and obviously across Europe and they appear to have been worshipped by early Gauls and Germanic tribes. The archaeological finds date between the 1st and 5th Century CE. All the inscriptions look to be thanks for prayers that had been answered. All of the images show three women, all seated and each wearing traditional Germanic style clothing, probably from the Ubii tribe. It seems they are all three of them, mothers. A Triple Goddess? All three of them slot into the mother role, but I don't think we know enough about them to make a definite call.

The Morrigan (sometimes called Anand or Anu), Badb and Macha

The Morrigan is an individual Irish deity or a collective title given to her and including her two sisters, Badb and Macha. This title also seems to sometimes cover the goddesses Fea and Nemain. But let's focus on Badb, Macha and Morrigu/Anand. Whatever way you look at it, the Morrigan is a war goddess. She is a complicated deity and one that I couldn't hope to even touch on the edges of within this paragraph, if you are drawn to her I do encourage you to do some research. As well as her sisters Badb and Macha, she also associated with the three goddesses Banba, Fotla and Eriu. The Morrigan can be seen in many guises, as crow or raven but also anything from a young woman to a crone and different animals as well. Macha also seems to have many guises but is often described as a Queen, but she does appear to have a strong connection to the land, fields and farming. Badb is another shape shifter, depicted as a crone or a young woman and in the form of a crow. She has a strong connection with the colours of black, white and red.

The suggestion has been made that Morrigan is the goddess representing sovereignty, Badb is the warrior of battle and Macha covers fertility, making them a triplicity. A triple goddess? Not in the known sense, because I think each of these goddesses are a triple energy individually.

The Norns; Urd, Verdandi, Skuld

From Norse mythology come the Norns (pronounced norms). They control and create the fate of the cosmos. The original belief was that there were many of them within this group, some descending from the gods and others from the elves or the dwarves. Then we come to the poem Voluspa, which gives the idea of the three Norns we are familiar with.

The three Norns are Urd who represents the past, Verdandi who is the present and Skuld who is the future. They live beneath Yggdrasil, the tree of life which hosts the entrance to the Nine Worlds within its branches and roots. Perhaps not identified specifically as goddesses, so not really as a Triple Goddess, but they certainly fit an interesting pattern.

Oshun, Oba, Oya

Orishas from the Yoruba tradition. The link for these three is that they all seem to be wives of Shango, the Yoruba god of thunder. Oba is the senior wife, then Oshun, with Oya as the junior. Oba is a river spirit and represents time and life. Oya is the Orisha of winds in all forms. Oshun is the Orisha of fresh water, fertility and love. She creates life but also has the power to destroy too. Perhaps loosely in the form of a Triple Goddess?

Parvati, Lakshmi, Saraswati

Three Hindu deities bound in a trinity by the fact they are consorts to the Divine Trinity of Indian gods, Brahma, Vishnu and Shiva.

Lakshmi is the goddess of wealth, prosperity and generosity. She helps her followers to achieve their goals and brings them abundance. Usually depicted as a beautiful woman seated in a full blooming lotus flower, surrounded by elephants. Lakshmi in

36

turn has eight manifestations of herself, eight sources of wealth and power.

Parvati is the ultimate female divinity. She is a gentle mother goddess but is also known for stepping up and releasing her power and strength when the need arises. The stories tell that Parvati is mother to the elephant headed god, Ganesha. Like Lakshmi, Parvati also has different aspects, one of those being as a warrior goddess.

Saraswati is the Hindu goddess of knowledge, the arts and learning. Often depicted as a beautiful pale skinned woman wearing all white, seated in a lotus with a swan present.

The Hindu myths and deities can become very complicated. It is a beautiful pantheon of deities but takes a while to research properly. Each one has many facets and individual ways of worship. These three are seen as a divine trinity.

Parvati, Durga, Kali Ma

I have mentioned Parvati above, but she has other forms, some of those are as Durga and Kali Ma. These forms are all worshipped as individual goddesses in their own right. Durga is a warrior goddess and called upon for protection, riding into battle and defeating evil astride her tiger, however she is also seen as mother to all. Kali is the destroyer goddess, fearsome and keeper of time, she is also a creator. Seen with blue or black skin and wearing skulls around her neck. Perhaps closer to the idea of a Triple Goddess, but these deities are so much more.

Sirens/Seirenes

From Greek mythology we have another set of three, this time they are sea nymphs that lure sailors to their deaths with bewitching songs. When Persephone was taken by Hades, the goddess Demeter gave three of Persephone's handmaidens the ability to fly. She gave them the bodies of birds. This was to enable them to help look for Persephone. It seems they got bored searching and flew off to set up home on the island of Anthemoessa. Often seen in images with the upper bodies of women but the legs of birds. Not quite what we recognize as a mermaid? A Triple Goddess? No, I think not.

The Thriae/Thriai

Who knew there were deities with the bodies of bees? The ancient Greek myths are full of surprises. The Thriai are three nymphs who worked with the art of prophecy using pebbles and birds of omen. Images show them with the heads of women and the bodies of bees, which is quite a bizarre picture.

Another set of three, but another to strike from the Triple Goddess list?

Tlazolteotl

Every so often you discover a goddess that raises your eyebrows, Tlazolteotl is one of them. A goddess of the Aztecs she covered sexual impurity and sinful behaviour. I love that they have a goddess for every occasion. She was an earth mother goddess and seen in four different stages; that of a young carefree temptress, a goddess of gambling with a destructive streak, a middle age goddess whose purpose was to forgive human sins and a scary crone with a destructive nature. The four aspects are seen as sisters; Tiacapan, Teicu, Tlaco and Zocutzin, all were apparently very adept at tempting people towards sin.

The name Tlazolteotl translates as 'earth, filth or dirt goddess'. She is also known as goddess of the Witches (let's not even begin to wonder what the connection there is…). She also appears in other aspects as Tlaelcuani, the Eater of Filth, Teteoinnan, Mother of the Gods and Toci, Grandmother who heals. Definitely an interesting deity. I think the last three aspects are why she often appears in suggestions of a Triple Goddess.

The Zorya

A Slavic goddess seen as one, two or three aspects. As one goddess she is the goddess of dawn and her sister, Danica is the goddess of dusk. Other stories tell of her as one goddess that represents three aspects, the morning, evening and night. In this triple aspect she is a virgin, a mother and an old woman. This works for me as a Triple Goddess example within one deity.

Working with the Triple Goddess

Within this section I have broken down the goddesses into four phases. You can choose to work with one, two, three or all four of them. It doesn't matter which or what order, the choice must be yours. In all honesty the choice is probably hers, because the Goddess speaks loudly and will continue to hassle you until you listen. I have used female pronouns because I work with the Goddess as a strong feminine energy. But as a reminder, she does have masculine energies too. You can work with the Goddess in whatever way suits you. Feminine energy can be anywhere between gentle new beginnings, nurturing, supportive, forgiving and loving right through to dark inner work, creation and aspects of death and rebirth. Every single one of us no matter what gender, sex, race, colour or creed carries feminine energy within. How you choose to work with that is up to you.

You may feel the call of the Goddess, you might feel that you are in desperate need of her guidance. You may be mildly interested, or you might believe that you are spiritually and mentally fully rounded and need only a little guidance or assistance. Personally, I believe we all go through phases in life, those of spiritual and mental growth along with physical changes. Each stage produces its own issues, obstacles and hopefully, also, revelations. You could sail through life with little to hinder your way. Most of us though, deal with problems on a regular basis. Working with the Goddess energy can in some way help, it might be on a spiritual level or she could play a huge supporting role. I wholeheartedly believe that we are always learning, no one person can ever know everything. There are always new pathways to take and new adventures or interests to take onboard.

Even if you have been on a spiritual pathway for many years, sometimes it is beneficial to go back to basics, not for a complete reset but just as a refresher. If you are starting your spiritual journey from scratch, oh my, what a wonderful adventure you have in front of you!

There are no benchmarks, no judgements about how far you have come or how much you have learnt, each journey is very personal and individual. There are also no direct routes or short cuts to experience. Each person will take a different journey, and each journey will usually be incredibly wiggly, it will spiral, bend, twist and turn in all kinds of directions. Go with the flow...

Working with the Goddess can provide you will all sorts of healing and self-discovery. I can promise you it will be interesting, exciting and amazing but I warn you it will probably include some messy stuff along the way, the Goddess knows how to kick some serious butt.

You won't find what I call 'womb work' within this book, that just isn't my style (and I am not dissing it or anyone that does it). If you are seeking more womb centric works then there are lots of books out there on the subject. I prefer to work with something that is more open to all. Whether you have a womb or not, should not in my opinion affect how you work with the Goddess or indeed magic or Witchcraft as a whole.

I don't care who you are, what you are or what you identify as (that's your business), neither in my opinion does the Goddess, she does not discriminate. Trust is key here, trust your own intuition, it won't let you down. You have the power within, let the Goddess guide you, but do make the most of your journey, it will be enlightening.

Calling upon her

There are many ways to call upon the Goddess in her particular phases and as many if not more reasons for doing so. It may be that you chose a particular phase of her to help you with a period or issue that is happening in your own life. You may need to step back from working so hard and let out your inner child, calling upon the maiden aspect would be perfect for that. If you need some support with a family situation or issue at home, then the mother aspect would probably be the best one to ask for guidance. A work situation that requires some tough decisions may benefit from the matriarch energy. Dealing with inner work, past life issues or something that you need to let go would be best dealt with by working with crone energy. There are cross overs between them all obviously, trust your intuition on which one to work with, or listen, the Goddess will probably make a suggestion for you. You can also work with them for magic. For instance, a spell for a new business would benefit from the fresh new beginning's energy of the maiden, but you could then move on with the spell and call upon any of the other phases of Goddess to help you with each stage of the business set up and structure. Calling upon more than one will help you with each of their levels of experience.

The Maiden

The maiden is usually thought of as a virgin but we need to remember that the original meaning of the word virgin meant someone who was free and not married, rather than someone who had not had sex before. A youngling, one who is perhaps unaware of her potential but full of ideas, energy and enthusiasm. We all start here, with the maiden energy. The innocent and excitement of youth, perhaps a little naïve, but open to all kinds of possibilities with no preconceptions. This is a phase where we set our foundations for life.

How does that relate to our current times though? You don't usually see fair maidens with flowers in their flowing hair dancing down the high street ... at least not where I live. I guess the modern-day equivalent would be a group of teenagers walking home from school carrying their books in fashionable hand bags, mobile phone in the other hand, wearing makeup and talking about who is seeing what boy and what the latest gossip is. That isn't to say the youth of today is bad, I have teenage children myself and am a very proud mother.

My own youth was in the eighties, a time of ra ra skirts, leg warmers and electronic pop music and I loved every minute of it, my teenage years played a huge part in shaping the person that I am today (and yes, I still wear leg warmers).

To me the maiden Goddess isn't about floaty dresses and running through fields of corn with wild abandon (although you can if you want to), it is about remembering that you were young once. Reminding yourself that you made rash choices based on all sorts of outside influences but also that you had fun, you had few worries (apart from what to wear to the Friday night disco) looking back life was totally care free, although it probably didn't seem so at the time, ask my parents...I had my fair share of dramas! But although I wouldn't want to go back to being 16 (I like being a grown up and being able to make my own life decisions) and although I wouldn't mind the figure that I had then...I learnt very valuable life lessons from those years and it is good to look back and remember how I dealt with certain situations and how good it felt to just dance, laugh and let some situations just sort themselves out without getting involved in all the drama.

Alternative name suggestions
- Spring
- East
- Air
- Waxing
- Sunrise
- Fields
- Youth
- Carefree
- Youngling
- Warrior

- Student
- Innocent
- Seed
- Act One
- Dark
- Energetic
- Child
- Pioneer
- Primary
- Beginnings
- Fresh
- Princess
- Adventurer
- Huntress

Her attributes and the areas of magic she can help you with

- Anticipation
- Balance
- Beauty
- Carefree
- Creation
- Curiosity
- Dawn
- Desires
- Discovery
- Enchantment
- Enthusiasm
- Exploration
- Hope
- Huntress
- Independence
- Initiation
- Innocence
- Inspiration

- Intelligence
- Naivety
- Nature
- New beginnings
- Play
- Pleasure
- Potential
- Purity
- Self-Awareness
- Self Confidence
- Self-Expression
- Sexuality
- Skill
- Spirituality
- Spring
- Trust
- Understanding
- Vitality
- Your Inner Child
- Youth

Maiden Goddesses

I have given brief descriptions for each and the magic you can call upon each goddess to assist you with. If you feel drawn to any of them, I strongly recommend doing your homework on them properly first. Do some research, read their stories and myths and learn about their characters before working with them.

Airmid/Airmed – A Celtic (Ireland) Goddess of healing. She was skilled with both magic and herbalism. She also covered learning and relationships. Her name translates as 'measure of grain'. Her father is the healing God Dian Cecht. The story tells that Airmid found herbs growing on the grave of Miach (he replaced the silver arm of Nuada with one of flesh and blood). She laid them all out on her cloak to learn their properties. There were 365 of them, to cover every possible ailment. Call upon Airmid for healing, learning, relationships, magic, herbalism.

Al-Uzza – A pre-Islamic goddess from Arabia who is sometimes referred to as one of the daughter's of Al-Lah (the God). She is the goddess of the morning and evening star and her name translates as 'the mighty one'. She is a strong goddess who oversees both love and war. The title 'Chaamu' was used for her in the 4th Century by St Epiphanius, this translates as 'young girl' or 'virgin' so she fits quite nicely into the Maiden role. Call upon Al-Uzza for love, strength, victory.

Ariadne – A Greek, more exactly a Minoan goddess from Crete, who was married to the Greek god of wine, Dionysos. She appears in a lot of images beside her husband feasting and dancing. Some stories say that she helped the Athenian hero, Theseus, escape from the Labyrinth after he slew the Minotaur. Theseus then abandoned her and at that point Dionysus rescued her, going on to have several children with him and eventually ascending to Olympus with him. Other tales tell of her being killed by the goddess Artemis. Call upon Ariadne for love, marriage, childbirth, addictions.

Artemis – A Greek Olympian goddess of the hunt. She also covers wild animals, woodlands, forests and protects childbirth and young girls. On the flip side she can also bring death and disease to women. Her brother Apollo deals with the men. In most ancient images of Artemis, she is seen holding a bow and arrow and depicted as a young maiden/late teen. This gal is totally independent and a good lass to call upon when you need some warrior energy. Call upon Artemis for warrior energy, protection, independence, defense, childbirth, hunting (not just animals, but when you are searching for anything).

Blodeuwedd – A Welsh deity known as the flower face goddess, because that's how she was created, from flowers. Magicians created her from bean, broom, meadowsweet, primrose, burdock, nettle, oak, hawthorn and chestnut blossoms. Married to the sun god Lugh she was then unfaithful; the punishment was for the same Magicians to turn her into an owl. She is the maiden, a goddess of spring, beauty (albeit temporary), death and omens. Call upon Blodeuwedd for relationships, hope, beauty, charity, help, support.

Brighid – a fiery Irish goddess whose name translates as authority, strength and power. She is seen as an individual deity but also as three sisters, each with the same name. She is goddess of poetry, smithcraft and healing. Her father is the Dagda. She protects sacred wells and healing rivers. Call upon Brighid for healing, inspiration, power, strength, courage, rebirth, creativity.

Chalchihuitlicue – An Aztec goddess whose name translates as 'she who wears a green/jade skirt'. She rules rivers, lakes, streams and all fresh water. In Aztec myth she was ruler of the fourth of the previous suns. Aztec myths describing the world as five suns (or creations), the first four of which relate to the elements, the fourth one being water. She apparently destroyed the fourth sun by bringing about torrential rain to cause a flood. She did however spare humans by transforming them into fish so they would not drown. The use of corn is attributed to her. Her rule also includes childbirth, protection of children and fertility. Call upon Chalchihuitlicue for fertility, childbirth, water magic, emotions, cleansing, purification, protection, creativity, inspiration.

Diana – a Roman goddess and Queen of Witches. Her name

derives from the Latin 'dium' meaning sky and 'dius' meaning daylight. Originally, she was Queen of the skies but eventually took on a lot of similarities with Artemis, becoming a hunting goddess. Call upon Diana for fertility, abundance, harvest, children, moon magic, water magic, protection, nurturing, forests, animals, sun magic.

Flora – A Roman goddess of spring, dancing, singing, drinking and flowering plants. She not only deals with blossoming flowers but also blossoming girls as they transition into being a woman. Her name is derived from the Latin word 'floris' which means 'a flower' but it also carries the meaning of 'in its prime'. She has her own festival, the Floralia which is held when the flowers are all in bloom mid-spring. Her images show her as a maiden, wearing light clothing and always holding or wearing flowers. Call upon Flora for fertility, spring, sex, transitions, garden magic.

Freya – A Norse goddess of love, beauty, sex, fertility, poetry and seidr (seership). She also covers war, because why wouldn't you? Often seen as the most beautiful of all goddesses, apparently no man or god could resist her. She is Queen of the Valkyries gathering souls of the dead from the battle fields. Freya happens to be a mad cat lady, owning a golden chariot that is drawn by two cats, you have to give her credit for the skill in training two cats to pull a chariot... Her name translates as 'the lady'. Call upon Freya for love, beauty, sex, fertility, poetry, divination, psychic abilities, Otherworld connection.

Hebe – Here we have a goddess of youth from the Greek pantheon. She is a cupbearer for the gods and serves ambrosia at the heavenly feasts. Also, an attendant to the goddess Aphrodite, she looks after young brides. Some stories tell that she stopped being a cupbearer because she married the god Hercules, others say she was fired after tripping over and revealing herself when her dress slipped – ooops. Hebe also apparently looked after the fountain of youth. She has an opposite in the form of a daimon (personified spirit) called Geras, he is the spirit of old age and a malevolent one at that. Her Roman name is Juventas. Call upon Hebe for youth, inner child, weddings, strength, energy.

Kore – This Greek maiden goddess was originally called Kore and then after marrying Hades she became known as Persephone. She is described in the stories as a beautiful maiden, kidnapped by Hades and taken to the Underworld to be his wife. I wonder if perhaps in her maiden role she is Kore, but once she is married to Hades and becomes Persephone, she loses some of her maiden qualities? After she ate pomegranate seeds, she was tied to the Underworld but only for half of the year. When she comes back to the earth, she brings spring and then summer with her. Then when she descends it becomes autumn then winter. Call upon Kore for cycles of all types but particularly of birth, life and death, spring, luck, youth, energy, good fortune, beauty.

Ostara/Eostre – A Germanic goddess of spring, fertility and rebirth. Stories also describe her as goddess of dawn and new beginnings. She is mentioned in ancient writings by Bede the Monk, suggesting that during Eostremonath, which is the Anglo-Saxon name for April, Pagans celebrated and held festivals in her honour. There is very little information about her, was she a goddess at all, or perhaps a variation on another deity? Who knows for sure? She certainly embodies the energy of spring and all the aspects of a maiden. Call upon Ostara for fertility, spring, rebirth, renewal, new beginnings, hope.

Nimue – (pronounced NIY-Muw-ey, neem-way, nee-moo-eh-eh) an interesting goddess with many variations on her story. She is also known as Lady of the Lake, the 'moistened bint' (excuse the

Monty Python reference) who handed the sword to Arthur. Her name is seen as Nimue or Vivienne. Nimue could be a variation on Mnemosyne, one of the nine water nymph Muses. She is connected with the ancient British goddess Coventina, possibly one and the same deity. Nimue was a student of the great sorcerer Merlin and also his lover. Morgan le Fay taking over at some point, perhaps they are aspects of the same goddess? She was believed to have been one of the three Queens who escorted Arthur to Avalon. Call upon Nimue for water magic, knowledge, wisdom, magic.

Persephone or Proserpina - see Kore (above)

Rhiannon – As well as being the name of a well-known Fleetwood Mac song (bet you are singing it now). Rhiannon is a Welsh goddess, sometimes connected with the Gaulic Epona and the ancient British goddess Rigantona. Very much associated with horses, particularly white ones. She was married to Pwyll, a chieftain of Dyfed but failed to produce a child for many years, Pwyll blamed Rhiannon and mistreated her because of it. Eventually she gave birth to a son, Pryderi although local gossip accused her of devouring him (yuck! and untrue). She makes an appearance in the Mabinogion. Although I have included her in the Maiden section, I think Rhiannon has aspects of all of the phases within her. She is maiden, but also mother, queen and with her Otherworld connection, she is also crone. Call upon Rhiannon for movement, communication, relaxation, fertility, leadership, productivity, moon magic, Otherworld, death, dreams, patience, sex, prosperity, divination, self-confidence, transformation.

Thalia – A song, music and dance goddess belonging to the nine Greek muses. Looking for comedy, poetry and a good time? Then Thalia is your gal. Her name means 'luxurious and grand banquets'. She is all about youth, beauty, happiness, richness, luxury, festivities and celebrations. Her name is also said to mean 'the blooming' which could be a reference to springtime. Call upon Thalia for youth, beauty, happiness, luxury, spring, abundance.

Maiden correspondences
Moon phase: New waxing
Season: Spring
Direction: East
Element: Air

Herbs, plants and foods
Trust your intuition when choosing what ingredients to work with for this phase of the Goddess. However, here are my suggestions based on the qualities this facet of the Goddess brings:

African violet, alyssum, avocado, banana, bay, beech, beetroot, benzoin, butter, birch, black pepper, camellia, caraway, chamomile, cherry, chrysanthemum, cinnamon, cowslip, crab, crocus, cucumber, dates, dill, dogwood, eggs, elm, fennel, frankincense, grapes, hawthorn, hazel, heliotrope, holly, honey, honeysuckle, ice cream, lamb, liquorice, mango, milk, mushrooms, mustard, oak, olives, orchid, oysters, patchouli, peach, pennyroyal, pomegranate, plum, rowan, rue, self-heal, soya, star anise, sweet pea, thyme, vanilla, vervain, willow, wine, witch hazel, woodruff, yogurt.

Crystals
Again, go with your intuition on this and what you have available. A small tumble stone crystal is just as magical as a large, more expensive piece. And natural items all have magic within, if all you have to hand is a pebble or a shell then that

will work perfectly. However, if you like to work with crystals, here are my suggestions to correspond with this phase of the Goddess:

Agate (blue lace), agate (moss), agate, amber, amethyst, aventurine (green), bloodstone, calcite (orange), celestite, chrysocolla, chrysoprase, copper, fluorite, garnet, gold, goldstone, hematite, Howlite, jasper, kyanite, labradorite, lapis lazuli, larimar, lepidolite, moonstone, obsidian (black), pyrite, quartz, quartz (rose), quartz (smoky), rhodonite, rhodochrosite, selenite, serpentine, silver, sodalite, sugilite, sunstone, tiger's eye, tourmaline, turquoise, unakite.

Modern Meet the Maiden Meditation

I have given a meditation here that shows the maiden in a more modern situation. Make yourself comfortable in a space where you won't be disturbed. Close your eyes and focus on your breathing, deep breaths in and deep breaths out.

As your world around you dissipates you find yourself standing outside a coffee shop in a small village street. Someone walks past you and enters the café. As the door opens you are met with the scent of delicious coffee and sweet cakes. You follow them in.

It is quite busy with most of the tables already taken but you head to the counter at the back of the café. A huge array of tantalizing treats is spread out in the cabinet in front of you, cakes, cookies and sweet treats of every description. A blackboard on the wall above also shows a large choice of both hot and cold drinks. The person behind the counter asks what you would like, and you place your order. As they get it ready for you, turn and take a look around the café. So many different people all happily chatting and enjoying their fare.

One person catches your eye, a teenager sitting on their own at a table by the window, head down, concentrating on the screen of their mobile phone. Opposite them seems to be the only free chair in the café.

Taking your tray with your food and drink you head over towards them. You ask if the seat is taken and they look up, distractedly but gesture for you to sit down.

As you sip your drink and eat your food you gaze out of the window and watch everyone as they walk past, each one in a world of their own.

A voice disrupts your thoughts and you realise the teenager has asked you to pass the sugar. You hand the bowl over.

You ask if they are waiting for someone to join them. The reply is they will catch up with their friends in a short while, but they like to come into the café for cake.

A conversation begins, you ask questions about their life and they reply. Then they ask you about your situation and you find yourself sharing.

Listen to the replies, the words, they are wise beyond their years. You are encouraged to remember your teenage years, the freedom, the energy and a young perspective on life in general.

When the conversation starts to wane their phone pings, and they thank you for the chat, but they need to leave to meet their friends. You thank them for sharing and their time as they get up and head out of the door.

You finish your drink and cake and then get up and make your way out until you are standing on the pavement outside once again.

Remember what you talked about and think about how you could implement some of the suggestions into your life to bring a younger perspective.

When you are ready slowly and gently come back to this reality. Wriggle your fingers and toes, open your eyes. Have something to eat and drink.

A Ritual of Beginnings

The maiden energy can help you discover what you really want, what you really, really want (no apologies made for the song words reference...). She can help you recognise what blockages are stopping you from doing what you want to in life. And also, to create the best version of you possible, if that's the direction you want to go. It will hopefully open up a pathway of discovery and help you begin a new adventure in your life. Well, it will be a step in the right direction anyway, you are the one that must do the leg work.

You will need:
Candles and safe holders or symbols for each quarter if using
Lighter
Incense (optional)
Something comfortable to sit or lie on
A drum or meditation music (optional)
A crystal for new beginnings, I would suggest a moss agate, kyanite or moonstone but go with what you have, what you are drawn to or pick one from the suggested maiden crystal list in this book.

Cast your circle by walking deosil (clockwise), if you are limited for space, stand and turn around on the spot. Visualise a circle of light surrounding you and then going above and below to form a sphere. If you have the room, you could sprinkle dried herbs or flowers to create the circle. If you are outside, please don't use anything that is not biodegradable. Say:
Goddess power to create a round
With maiden energy this circle is bound

Call in the quarters. This can be done completely with visualisation, but you could also light a candle for each direction. As you call each quarter see and feel the qualities of that element. Or you might like to place items at each compass point, such as a bowl of salt for north/earth, incense for east/air, a candle for south/fire and a bowl of water for west/water.

Turn to the East and say:
> *Element of air with your intellect and wisdom I invite you to join my rite today. Welcome!*

Turn to the South and say:
> *Element of fire with your passion and creativity I invite you to join my rite today. Welcome!*

Turn to the West and say:
> *Element of water with your intuition and emotions I invite you to join my rite today. Welcome!*

Turn to the North and say:
> *Element of earth with your grounding and stability I invite you to join my rite today. Welcome!*

Call in the maiden. I have chosen Rhiannon for this ritual but be guided by whichever goddess you feel will work for you.

> *I call upon the beautiful goddess Rhiannon, in your guise as maiden And ask that you join me today and lend your energies of self-confidence, new beginnings and discovery to my rite. Welcome!*

Light some incense if you wish and drum or put on some soft music. Sit or lie down comfortably. Take your chosen crystal and hold it in your hand. Feel a connection to the energy of the crystal. Close your eyes and focus on your breathing, deep breaths in and deep breaths out.

> *As your world around you dissipates you find yourself standing on the side of a hill. Soft, lush grass is growing beneath your feet and*

the fields and hills around you are covered in green, speckled with pretty wildflowers.

The sky above you is a clear blue and the sun is warm but fresh, with a gentle breeze.

As you are admiring your surroundings you hear a noise and turn to see what looks like a white horse bearing a rider in the distance. They are headed your way.

You watch as the horse majestically gallops towards you. As they come closer you see that the rider is a beautiful woman, dressed in white robes with her long blonde hair flowing behind her in the breeze.

When they draw near to you, she pulls up the horse to a stop and dismounts. The horse neighs softly and lowers its head to munch happily on the grass.

The woman walks towards you and introduces herself as Rhiannon. She holds out her hands and you respond, as your hands touch you feel a strong connection.

She invites you to walk with her, leading you further down the hill to a still pool of water that is fed by a local spring from above.

Rhiannon gestures for you to sit beside the pool.

For a while you sit in silence, watching the reflections on the water and just enjoying the surroundings.

Rhiannon then asks you to look at your own reflection in the pool, she asks what you see…

Not just what you see on the outside but to go deeper.

"What sort of person do you want to be? "

"What changes would you make in your life?"

"What new adventure would you like to start?"

Answer her questions honestly.

When you are finished Rhiannon asks you to look in the pool again and see if you can find solutions or changes that can be made or what needs to be done to make these new pathways happen.

Watch and listen very carefully…

Words or images may come from the pool, Rhiannon may have some

wisdom and insight to share with you too…
Once you are finished you both stand and Rhiannon hugs you
warmly. She also hands you a gift, take note of what she gives you.
She walks beside you back to her patiently waiting horse. She hugs
you again before mounting the white mare, turning and riding back
the way she came.
Think about what you have seen and heard and the meaning behind
the gift you were given.

Slowly and gently come back to this reality, wriggle your fingers
and toes and open your eyes. Eat and drink something. If you
are outside don't forget to share some of your drink or food to
the earth as a blessing.

Thank Rhiannon:
I give my thanks to the beautiful goddess Rhiannon, in your guise
as maiden
For joining me today and lending your energies of self-confidence,
new beginnings and discovery to my rite. Go if you must but stay
if you will.
With my gratitude and thanks, farewell.

Thank the quarters:
Turn to the North and say:
Element of earth with your grounding and stability I thank you for
joining my rite today. Farewell!

Turn to the West and say:
Element of water with your intuition and emotions I thank you for
joining my rite today. Farewell!

Turn to the South and say:
Element of fire with your passion and creativity I thank you for
joining my rite today. Farewell!

Turn to the East and say:
> *Element of air with your intellect and wisdom I thank you for joining my rite today. Farewell!*

Close the circle by walking widdershins (anti-clockwise) around your circle or turn around on the spot. Visualise the sphere dissipating and the circle disappearing. Say:
> *Goddess power dissolve this circle round*
> *With thanks for the maiden energy this circle is unwound*

The Mother

I guess the period from maiden to mother can vary greatly now, our ancestors would have had children at quite a young age – yes, I know that happens now, everyone has their own journey. I came to motherhood fairly late really, in my early 30s and actually it was the right time for me, I had no desire to be a mother until I hit the milestone of thirty and then panic set in as the biological clock started to tick incessantly loudly.

When I think about the word 'mother', I am probably visualising the stereotypical mother figure, slightly plump and wearing an apron with flour on her hands from making bread... yes, I know that is so outdated! There probably aren't many goddesses that wear aprons either. For reference my mother is very smart and fashionable, but also a wonderful cook. When I first became a mother I also worked in an office and believed that to be a mother I had to be perfect – a perfect wife, perfect mother, perfect home maker and also perfect at work...believe me it doesn't work, there just aren't enough hours in the day, trying to do it all is incredibly stressful there has to be some compromise. The key (for me anyway) in the mother stage is to not beat yourself up, having a dust free house is not a high priority when you have small children. I suspect although they didn't have the same outside influences, even our ancestors sometimes found motherhood stressful, worrying about the cold or the damp and whether there was enough food to feed all the hungry mouths. Sadly, that still happens in parts of the world today.

I don't think to connect with the mother stage in your life that you need to have your own children. This part of your journey is perhaps just about being comfortable, feeling secure and knowing that you are working towards being happy with yourself and who you are. You may not have children, but you may have those that are dependent on you, dogs, cats, partners, friends or relatives. You could also see it as nurturing your inner child. The mother gives birth to the abundance on earth, she represents the fullness of life.

Alternative name suggestions
- Summer
- South
- Fire
- Full
- Midday
- Forests
- Experience
- Productive
- Provider
- Creator
- Nurturer
- Teacher
- Learned
- Seedling
- Act Two
- Shadow
- Fruitful
- Parent
- Source
- Origin

- Progenitor
- Procreator
- Duchess
- Care giver

Her attributes and the areas of magic she can help you with
- Abundance
- Balance
- Caring
- Confidence
- Discipline
- Fertility
- Fruition
- Fulfilment
- Giving
- Growth
- Guidance
- Happiness
- Harmony
- Healing
- Help
- Ideas
- Love
- Marriage
- Nourishment
- Nurturer
- Patience
- Power
- Procreation
- Protection
- Provider
- Receiving
- Regeneration
- Relationships

- Responsibility
- Self-Care
- Self-Discipline
- Self-Understanding
- Spirituality
- Summer
- Sustainability

Mother Goddesses

Al-Lat – from pre-Islamic Arabia she along with her sisters are sometimes believed to be the daughters of Al-Lah (the God). Her name translates as 'the Goddess' and she is seen to be the mother. Her name can be found in ancient texts as 'Mother of the Gods' and 'Greatest of All'. Seen as an Earth goddess she deals with all of nature, fertility, prosperity and the spring. Images found of her show a crescent moon and a sun disk. In Arabia the sun was though to be a feminine energy, it could well have been associated with Al-Lat. Call upon Al-Lat for spring magic, fertility, prosperity, sun magic, strength, abundance.

Aphrodite – One of the Greek Olympian goddesses she covers love, beauty, pleasure and procreation. She is believed to be the mother of all living beings and creator of all nature, which in my book gives her the status of a mother goddess. Some stories tell of her captivating beauty, so much so that she used this power to rule over all. She is generous to those that worship and follow her, but apparently quite unhappy when people neglect her, she rewards that with punishment. She seems to be quite a stroppy, I want my own way kinda gal who also likes to stir up a bit of chaos wherever she goes! Call upon Aphrodite for love, beauty, pleasure, vitality, fertility, independence, protection, chaos.

Arianrhod – A Welsh goddess who is often seen as the mother aspect of the trio that includes Blodeuwedd and Cerridwen.

Her name translates as 'silver wheel or disc'. She is strongly connected with the moon, as ruler of Caer Sidi she carries those who pass over to the heavens to help them reincarnate. She also has the ability to shapeshift into an owl allowing her to see all. Apparently Arianrhod had a thing for mermen, any mermen. However, her twin children were born magically, by leaping over a wizard's staff before they had come to full term. One fetus slipped away never to be seen again, the other was taken by Arianrhod's brother, Gwydion. Perhaps not the best example of motherhood...Call upon Arianrhod for death/rebirth, renewal, wisdom, moon magic, initiation, past lives, creation, the arts, manifesting.

Badb – A Celtic/Irish war and crow goddess (see The Morrigan info). Although not part of a triple goddess in the usual sense, she could be slotted into any of the roles. I have put her here in the mother section because she is said to use a cauldron in the Otherworld, the souls were popped into the cauldron and asked if they wanted to be reborn or not. I see the cauldron as a creation tool, one that fits with the mother phase. But you might think otherwise... Call upon Badb for enlightenment, inspiration, life, wisdom, divination, reincarnation, past lives.

Bast – Egyptian goddess of home, domestic life, secrets, fertility, childbirth and ah yes, mad cat lady. Daughter of the son god, Ra. Her name is seen as Bast or Bastet. She plays a very strong role in protection of all kinds. She is depicted as a good mother to her two children. Although her festivals involved drinking copious amounts of wine, don't all good mothers do that? Call upon Bast for fertility, childbirth, truth, home life, protection, motherhood.

Ceres – A Roman goddess of fertility, agriculture and the growing of food. She was worshipped and honoured to bring good grain harvests. She is patron to farmers and protector of the plebeians (a commoner). She seems to have been adapted from the Greek Demeter with a similar story, being mother to Proserpina who was abducted by Pluto. She gave guidance to the Tribune of Plebeians. She was a deity of the common people of Rome. Her name translates as 'to nourish, feed or to grow'. Call upon Ceres for growth, harvest, fertility, protection, truth, justice, abundance.

Corn Mother – The Corn Mother is an old woman found in tales from the indigenous tribes of North America. The story tells that she feeds her entire tribe by rubbing her body. As she does this, grains or corn are produced. However, once the tribe discover this is how she is providing their food, understandably they are less than impressed. For this, she is accused of working with Witchcraft and killed. After her body is buried it continues to produce corn. This is only one of the variations of the story, there are many others, but they all have the same theme, that of providing corn to keep the tribe fed and alive. She is also associated with children. Call upon the Corn Mother for abundance, prosperity, harvest, fertility, health, protection for children, grounding, healing, energy, strength, nurturing.

Cybele/Kybele – From Greece, she is the Phrygian Mother of all Gods, humans, animals and plant life (she must have been constantly exhausted). Worshipped as a primal nature goddess in central and western Anatolia. She was born to a sky god and earth goddess and came into life as a hermaphrodite, meaning that she is both male and female. The Gods were very unaccepting of this, so they castrated her, throwing the male organ onto the ground, from which grew an almond tree. Call upon Cybele for love, health, humour, victory, relationships, strength, earth magic, fertility, nature.

Danu – an Irish goddess. She is a mother and earth goddess, a creator of life. Some stories tell that she fought in the first battle of Maige Tuired alongside Macha, Badb and the Morrigan. It has been suggested that her name may be connected to the Danube River, giving her a water aspect as well as Earth Mother. Although the word 'danu' also means 'to flow'. She is mother to all the Tuatha De Danann. Call upon Danu for craftsmanship, music, poetry, magic, wisdom, power, inspiration, intellect, wealth, abundance.

Demeter – Greek Olympian goddess, Demeter looks after agriculture of all kinds including grain and bread. She takes charge of the Mystery Cults, taking initiates on their pathway to the realm of Elysium. Mother to Persephone, she obviously fits in the mother category of the Triple Goddess, but I also think she fits quite well into the matriarch phase as well. The last part of her name 'meter' translates generally as 'mother'. However, the 'de' part is disputed, some believe it could be associated with 'Gaea' making her Mother Earth, others suggest it is linked to 'Deo' which may have been the name of a particular type of grain. Call upon Demeter for harvest, abundance, protection, patience, love, devotion.

Frigg – From the Norse pantheon, Frigg (or Frigga) is the highest ranking of the Aesir goddesses, Queen of the Aesir. Mother to the god Baldur and married to the leader of the Norse gods, Odin – so she is pretty much in charge. As a völva (seeress/ sorceress), she practices the Norse magic of seidr, working with changes, fates and the power to weave new pathways. Her name translates as 'beloved'. Her domain also covers marriage, love and protection particularly in the home. Call upon Frigg for love, marriage, protection, crafts, divination, fate, peace, social order, diplomacy, motherhood, prophecy.

Gaia – Greek goddess of the earth. A protogenos (primordial

elemental deity) she was born at the very beginning of all creation. Hooking up with Ouranos/Uranus (sky) Pontos (sea), Gigantes (giants) and Tartaros (the Pit) all heavenly and sea gods, giants and mortal creatures were born from her. She was known for antagonizing the gods, rebelling and defying with most of the key players at one point or another. A fun fact – ancient Greeks believed the earth was a flat disk surrounded by the river Oceanus, with a dome (heaven) covering the top and a great pit below (Tartaros). Call upon Gaia for abundance, nature, earth magic, promises, divination, gratitude, providence, harvest, fertility.

Hathor – an Egyptian goddess. The sun god Ra plucked Hathor from Ureas' brow and sent her to earth in the form of a lion. This was all organised by Ra with the intention of Hathor punishing mankind for not obeying his laws. She created what can only be described as a blood bath. In an attempt to curb her blood lust Ra poured 7000 jugs of beer and pomegranate juice in her path. She took the bait and drunk the lot which caused her to fall asleep for three days. It seemed the plan worked. Obviously with that much beer inside her Hathor is known for the love of song and happiness. She also covers fertility and all of the good things in life. Hathor is seen as a goddess of the heavens and stars. Call on Hathor for love, feminine energy, beauty, happiness, sexuality, sky magic, romance, the arts, protection (particularly for women).

Hera – an Olympian Queen of the Gods from the Greek pantheon. Hera is the goddess of marriage, women and all the stars in the sky and the heavens. One story tells that Hera and her husband Zeus had an argument. She refused to speak to him. His way of winning her around was to dress up a wooden figure to look like a bride and declare he was going to marry it. Hera was understandably angry until she realized it was all a prank, and then apparently forgave him (I think I would have held out for wine and chocolates myself). Call upon Hera for love, romance, humour, forgiveness, creativity, marriages, relationships.

Isis – Egyptian goddess whose name derives from the word for 'throne', that tells you just how important she is. She was such an impressive goddess that her worship was not limited to Egypt and spread throughout the Roman empire and out to England and other far flung parts of the globe. Her parents are the earth god Gob and the sky goddess Nut. She was a fabulous Queen and taught her subjects how to brew, bake and weave (not necessarily in that order, or all at the same time). Call upon Isis for magic, dreams, divination, crafts, perspective, faithfulness, love, inner beauty, spirituality, destiny, harvest, fulfilment.

Juno – a Roman goddess she represented all aspects of womanhood, particularly married life and childbirth. Along with Jupiter and Minerva she forms the Capitoline triad of deities, which were introduced by the Etruscan kinds. Juno is mother to the god Mars. Call on Juno for love, relationships, leadership, feminine energy, protection of women and children, romance, friendship, leadership, moon magic.

Lakshmi – Lakshmi is the Hindu goddess of wealth, prosperity and generosity. She helps her followers to achieve their goals and brings them abundance. Usually depicted as a beautiful woman seated in a full blooming lotus flower, surrounded by elephants. Lakshmi in turn has eight manifestations of herself, eight sources of wealth and power. Call on Lakshmi for luck, wealth, relationships, prosperity, love, harvest, devotion, business matters.

Macha – an Irish goddess connected with the sovereignty of Ireland and the land. She is one of the Tuatha De Danann. Her sisters are Badb and the Morrigan. She appears in stories both as a fairy woman and a Queen. She is a warrior and a practitioner of magic. Call upon Macha for justice, protection for children and women, pregnancy, power, strength, magic.

Mary – from Christianity, Mary is perhaps one of the most famous mothers. She is mother of mankind and although technically no conception was involved, she gave birth to Jesus. She is obviously very much linked to miracles but also to the sun. Call on Mary for miracles, sun magic, blessings, prayers.

Parvati – From the Hindu pantheon, Parvati is the ultimate female divinity and married to the god Lord Shiva. She is a gentle mother goddess but is also known for stepping up and releasing her power and strength when the need arises. The stories tell that Parvati is mother to the elephant headed god, Ganesha. Like Lakshmi, Parvati also has different aspects, one of those being as a warrior goddess. Images of her often show Shiva by her side and a baby Ganesha on her lap. Call upon Parvati for love, family, marriage, parenthood, fertility, strength, determination, feminine energy, power.

Rhea - from the Greek pantheon, Rhea is Titaness mother of the gods. Her name translates as 'flow' and 'ease'. Her husband is Kronos. She represents the flow of time and of generations. This also represents the flow of menstrual blood, mother's milk and the waters of birth. She carries with her a huge powerhouse of female energy covering fertility and motherhood. Call upon Rhea for comfort, ease, fertility, feminine energy, pregnancy, birth, motherhood, going with the flow.

Selene – a Greek Titan goddess who is associated with the moon. Images of her usually include either a full moon or crescent symbol. Ancient Greek poets believed her to be the moon incarnate. Her brother, Helios is the sun and her sister, Eos is the dawn. Call upon Selene for all types of moon magic, emotions, peace, sleep, beauty, healing, rest.

Venus – a Roman goddess who was originally associated with gardens and cultivated fields. Her Greek counterpart is Aphrodite, the goddess of love. It seems she wasn't worshipped in early Roman times but found her way at some point. She was married to the god Vulcan and is mother to Cupid. Her history is one of romance and affairs with both gods and mortals, which seems ironic as she is a protector of chastity in women. Call upon Venus for love, romance, chastity, beauty, prosperity, fertility, victory.

Mother correspondences
Moon phase: Full
Season: Summer
Direction: South
Element: Fire

Herbs, plants and foods
Trust your intuition when choosing what ingredients to work with for this phase of the Goddess. However, here are my suggestions based on the qualities this facet of the Goddess brings:

African violet, agrimony, aloe, alyssum, anemone, angelica, apple, artichoke, ash, asparagus, aster, barley, basil, bay, benzoin, bergamot, betony, birch, blackberry, black pepper, blackthorn, bladder wrack, blueberry, bluebell, borage, bracken, broccoli, broom, Brussels sprouts, burdock, buttercup, cabbage, calamus, camellia, caraway, cardamom, carnation, cauliflower, cedar, celandine, chamomile, chicken, chickweed, chillies, chives, chrysanthemum, cinnamon, cinquefoil, clove, clover, coconut, coltsfoot, comfrey, copal, coriander, cornflower (batchelor's buttons), cowslip, cranberry, cramp bark, cucumber, cumin, curry leaves, cyclamen, cypress, daffodil, daisy, dandelion, datura, delphinium, dill, dittany of Crete; dock, dogwood, dragon's blood, dulse, echinacea, elder, elm, eucalyptus, fennel, fern, feverfew, fish, flax, foxglove, frankincense, garlic, geranium, ginger, gorse, gourd, grass, gravy, hawthorn, hazel, heather, heliotrope, holly, honey, honeysuckle, horehound, horseradish, hyacinth, hyssop, ivy, juniper, knotweed, lavender, leeks, lemon, lemon balm, liquorice, lilac, lily, lime, lobelia, lovage, lungwort, mallow, mandrake, maple syrup, marigold, marjoram, melon, mint, mistletoe, mugwort, mullein, mushrooms, mustard, myrrh, nettle, nutmeg, oak, olives, orchid, oysters, papaya, parsley, pasta, patchouli, pennyroyal, peony, periwinkle, pine, pineapple, pine nut, plantain, pomegranate, poppy seeds, potato, primrose, pumpkin, quince, radish, raspberry, rhubarb, rice, rose, rosemary, rowan, rue, saffron, sage, Saint John's Wort, salt, self-heal, sesame, snapdragon, Solomon's seal, sorrel, star anise, sugar, sunflower, sweetgrass, sweet pea, tansy, thistle, thyme, tobacco, tomato, tulip, turmeric, turnip, valerian, vervain, vinegar, violet, watercress, willow, witch hazel, woodruff, wormwood, yarrow.

Crystals

Again, go with your intuition on this and what you have available. A small tumble stone crystal is just as magical as a large, more expensive piece. And natural items all have magic within, if all you have to hand is a pebble or a shell then that will work perfectly. However, if you like to work with crystals, here are my suggestions to correspond with this phase of the Goddess:

Agate, agate (blue lace), agate (moss), amber, amethyst, aventurine (green), bloodstone, brass, calcite (orange), carnelian, celestite, chrysoprase, chrysocolla, citrine, copper, fluorite, garnet, gold, goldstone, hematite, Howlite, jade (nephrite), jasper, kyanite, labradorite, lapis lazuli, larimar, lepidolite, malachite, moonstone, obsidian (black), pebble, petrified wood, pyrite, quartz, quartz (rose), quartz (smoky), rhodochrosite, rhodonite, selenite, serpentine, silver, sodalite, sugilite, sunstone, tiger's eye, tourmaline, turquoise, unakite.

Modern Meet the Mother Meditation

I have given a meditation here that shows the mother in a more modern situation. Make yourself comfortable in a space where you won't be disturbed. Close your eyes and focus on your breathing, deep breaths in and deep breaths out.

As your world around you dissipates you find yourself standing outside a shop in a busy village street. In front of the shop windows are wooden benches stacked high with pot plants of all kinds. There are house plants, garden plants and herbs, each one beautiful.

The door opens with the tinkle of a bell and someone steps out carrying a large bouquet of flowers.

They hold the door open for you to step inside. Into a florist shop.

The walls either side are tiered with bucket upon bucket of fresh cut flowers of all varieties and colours.

As you take in your surroundings, the beauty of the flowers and the delicious scent from them, someone appears from the back and steps out from behind the counter.

Dressed in a bright coloured shirt and jeans with hair tied back in a ponytail they greet you and ask if they can help.

You stumble over your words because you don't know what you are there for.

They come over and start pointing out various flowers to you. They tell you their names and what folk meanings and associations they have.

They are quite talkative and begin to tell you about how they came to run the shop and how much they care about and love the flowers and plants. They talk about having a passion and something that really matters to them, encouraging you to do the same.

You begin to share your life situation too...

Listen to the replies, they may have some wise words for you.

Once you have finished talking you are asked if there is a particular flower you have seen that you like, and you point to one that has caught your attention.

They take out several stems and wrap them for you.

You go to your pocket to get out payment and they wave dismissively, telling you that it is a gift and no need to pay.

Thanking them for the flowers and their time you head back out of the shop.

Remember what you have talked about and what type of flower you chose.

Standing outside now on the pavement again, slowly and gently come back to this reality. Wriggle your fingers and toes and open your eyes. Have something to eat and drink. You might want to look up the magical properties and meaning of the flowers that you were given.

A Ritual of Self-Healing

The mother energy brings healing and nurturing. Whether it is emotional, mental or physical the energy of the mother goddess can bring you comfort and healing in many ways. Let her help you with any issues you have, lean into her support and strength and allow her to heal you or at least hold your hand whilst you do the work to heal yourself.

You will need:

Candles and safe holders or symbols for each quarter if using

71

Lighter
Incense (optional)
Something comfortable to sit or lie on
A drum or meditation music (optional)
A crystal for self-healing, I would suggest blue lace agate, fluorite, kyanite or rose quartz, but go with what you have, what you are drawn to or pick one from the suggested mother crystal list in this book.

Cast your circle by walking deosil (clockwise), if you are limited for space, stand and turn around on the spot. Visualise a circle of light surrounding you and then going above and below to form a sphere. If you have the room, you could sprinkle dried herbs or flowers to create the circle. If you are outside, please don't use anything that is not biodegradable. Say:
Goddess power to create a round
With mother energy this circle is bound

Call in the quarters. This can be done completely with visualisation, but you can also light a candle for each direction. As you call each quarter see and feel the qualities of that element. Or you could place items at each compass point, such as a bowl of salt for north/earth, incense for east/air, a candle for south/fire and a bowl of water for west/water.

Turn to the East and say:
Element of air with your intellect and wisdom I invite you to join my rite today. Welcome!

Turn to the South and say:
Element of fire with your passion and creativity I invite you to join my rite today. Welcome!

Turn to the West and say:

*Element of water with your intuition and emotions I invite you to
join my rite today. Welcome!*

Turn to the North and say:
*Element of earth with your grounding and stability I invite you to
join my rite today. Welcome!*

Call in the mother. I have chosen Parvati for this ritual but be
guided by whichever goddess you feel will work for you.

*I call upon the beautiful goddess Parvati, in your guise as mother.
And ask that you join me today and lend your energies of strength,
energy and determination to my rite.*
Welcome!

Light some incense if you wish and drum or put on some soft
music. Sit or lie down comfortably. Take your chosen crystal
and hold it in your hand. Feel a connection to the energy of
the crystal. Close your eyes and focus on your breathing, deep
breaths in and deep breaths out.

*As your world around you dissipates you find yourself standing in
a busy market.*
*You stand quietly and take in the scene around you. There are stalls
draped with beautiful silk fabrics and rugs of all colours, shapes
and sizes.*
*Vendors line the street selling a huge array of different spices and
herbs, set out in large sacks on the ground. Many of the tables are
covered in brightly coloured fresh fruit and vegetables.*
*Scents fill the air; rich spicy hot foot being cooked out on grills and
cups of hot milky spiced chai tea.*
*Once you have found your bearings you start to walk between
the stalls, watching and listening to all the life that is happening
around you. It has a wonderful lively happy energy that is buzzing.*

As you walk past each stall you spot an awning off to one side, this has gorgeous curtains of multi coloured fabric draped over the front to enclose the space. You are drawn to it.

Once you are outside the curtains are parted and a graceful and elegant woman steps out, gesturing for you to enter.

Walking through the curtains you arrive inside an exquisitely decorated space. Vibrant fabric hangs around the sides and above your head. The floor is covered with luxurious plump cushions in many colours.

The lady invites you to sit and make yourself comfortable.

She walks to what looks like an altar at one end of the space. It is covered with candles, gold statues of deities, flowers in all colours and you watch as she sprinkles a pinch of herbs onto a dish. As the herbs hit the charcoal inside the dish, smoke snakes upwards and a warm spicy scent begins to fill the air.

She turns and smiles at you, this is the goddess, Parvati.

Then she walks to one end of the altar and pours a cup of warm steaming liquid which she hands to you and you take. Sip it slowly. It is warm chai tea, hot milk infused with spices and honey. As you drink you feel the chai soothing and relaxing you. You lay back on the cushions.

Parvati begins to talk to you, she asks questions:

"What ails you in your body?"

"What ails you in your soul?"

"What ails you in your spirit?"

Take some time to think about the answers then reply to her.

She has some ideas and solutions for you, listen to them carefully.

When you have finished speaking, she takes the cup from you and then holds both of your hands. You can feel a connection, a healing and soothing energy washes over you.

Dropping your hands, she then places an item in the palm of one of them, it is a gift for you.

Then Parvati bids you farewell and reminds you that you can return to this place at any time.

You thank her and head out of the tent back into the street. The market holders are now packing up at the end of the day. The hustle and bustle has subsided and the area is beginning to quiet.

Walk back through the stalls and watch as they finish up, packing away all their wares.

Stop now and open your hand, take a look at the gift that Parvati gave you. What is it? What does it mean to you?

Think about what you have seen and heard and the meaning behind the gift you were given.

Slowly and gently come back to this reality, wriggle your fingers and toes and open your eyes. Eat and drink something. If you are outside don't forget to share some of your drink or food to the earth as a blessing.

Thank Parvati:

I give my thanks to the beautiful goddess Parvati, in your guise as mother.

For joining me today and lending your energies of strength, energy and determination to my rite. Go if you must but stay if you will. With my gratitude and thanks, farewell.

Thank the quarters:

Turn to the North and say:

Element of earth with your grounding and stability I thank you for joining my rite today. Farewell!

Turn to the West and say:

Element of water with your intuition and emotions I thank you for joining my rite today. Farewell!

Turn to the South and say:

Element of fire with your passion and creativity I thank you for joining my rite today. Farewell!

Turn to the East and say:
> *Element of air with your intellect and wisdom I thank you for joining my rite today. Farewell!*

Close the circle by walking widdershins (anti-clockwise) around your circle or turn around on the spot. Visualise the sphere dissipating and the circle disappearing. Say:
> *Goddess power dissolve this circle round*
> *With thanks for the mother energy this circle is unwound*

The Matriarch

I have put the matriarch stage in because I do feel that from mother to crone is such a big leap, if you are a mother you will always be a mother even when you are of crone age and even then, what age do you class as crone? If you have a child at the age of twenty, you could say you move out of the mother stage at forty perhaps? Which seems way too young to be a crone. This is where I see the matriarch stage fit in. The official meaning of matriarch is a leader of a clan or group, one that is a respected elder. I am not sure if there are any dedicated lists of matriarch Goddesses anywhere, probably not, I have included my suggestions here, but also take into consideration all the mother goddesses and even some of the crones, there is a cross over.

I think of this as the Autumn stage in your life, when you have achieved the goals you set in your early years, maybe you have a job that you have worked hard for, a nice house, nice car and all the material things if that is how you measure success. But also, from a spiritual point of view, I also believe that it is when a woman is maybe at her strongest point, she isn't young but isn't old, she is mature and knowledgeable, with good long-standing friends, confident in herself and able to deal with situations as they arise with wisdom and dignity...well hopefully anyway! This is perhaps also the period in a woman's life that she has a bit of spare cash and some time to herself to follow her dreams and wishes, to take up hobbies and maybe travel to places she has always wanted to see and discover more about herself in the process. On the downside this stage of life sees the beginning of the menopause but even then, perhaps it should be something that is celebrated as a rite of passage. And yes, I absolutely understand it could be hard to wrap your head around that idea, trust me.

Alternative name suggestions
- Autumn
- West
- Water
- Waning
- Sunset
- Ocean
- Maturity
- Independent
- Organiser
- Protector
- Wise One
- Teacher
- Sapling
- Queen
- Act Three
- Mists
- Productive
- Achiever
- Dignity
- Grande Dame

Her attributes and the areas of magic she can help you with
- Achievements
- Authority

- Autumn
- Confidence
- Control
- Dignity
- Dreams
- Experience
- Goals
- Knowledge
- Maturity
- Organisation
- Power
- Self Fulfilment
- Spirituality
- Success
- Travel
- Wisdom

Matriarch Goddesses

This section is really a case of personal choices. I think a lot of the mother goddesses would slot into this phase and some of the crone goddesses too. I have included a few suggestions of my own but trust your own intuition as to which goddesses you believe step over into this phase as well.

Durga – Durga is a Hindu warrior goddess and called upon for protection, riding into battle and defeating evil astride her lion or tiger, however she is also seen as mother to all. She was created for the very purpose of destroying the buffalo demon, Mahisasura. She takes on the collective energy, the shakti of male and female power. This is one kick ass deity. Call upon Durga for strength, justice, compassion, peace, calm, order, organization, destruction, dealing with conflict, protection.

Lilith – often seen as a demon goddess she hails from Sumaria and Babylon. She is probably best known from Jewish stories as being Adam's first wife, before Eve came along. She refused to obey his orders and left him, so we have the very first divorce! However, her actions resulted in her being cursed to give birth to one hundred demon children every day, each one was then killed. Her name translates as 'night creature'. Jewish folk stories tell of her as a succubus or a demon that arrives during the night to prey on young men. In more recent times she has come to be recognised as a strong independent woman who is totally comfortable with her own sexuality and refuses to be told what to do…go Lilith! Call upon Lilith for freedom, courage, passion, pleasure, sexuality, power, courage, independence.

Ereshkigal – from Mesopotamia, this goddess rules the 'Great Place or Great Below' the home of the dead. She not only looks after the dead but keeps a watchful eye on those that break the law and is the fount of life. Her servant is Namtar, the evil demon, Death, but who also happens to be her son. Ereshkigal also has the power to exorcise evil spirits from those who are sick. She did work her way through three consorts before the fourth one, Nergal agreed to stay with her. She is a dark goddess and one that can really help you work with your shadow side. Call upon Ereshkigal for shadow work, strength, emotions, understanding, support, knowledge, discovery, spiritual growth.

Inanna – Often referred to as Lady of the Heavens, this title has been bestowed on several different deities. In Sumeria she is Inanna, in the Akkadian Empire she is Ishtar and the Canaanite people know her as Astarte. At some point Inanna become Ishtar, a name that originates from Attar/Ashtart. Seemingly at this point she also gained the addition of male attributes. Inanna is daughter of the moon and the morning and evening star. Inanna goes into the underworld to learn about death and rebirth. Call upon Inanna for death and rebirth, knowledge, wisdom, love, passion, creativity, compassion, forgiveness, awareness, peace, unity, leadership.

Gorgons – A set of three winged daimones from Greece, the most famous one being Medusa or Medousa. Her two perhaps less well-known sisters are Sthenno and Euryale. Medusa is a beautiful woman who slept with the god Poseidon. This caused the goddess Athena to become angry, she was the one responsible for turning Medusa into a gorgon as punishment. Although some stories believe Medusa was born a gorgon, I will leave the choice up to you. Sthenno and Euryale were immortal beings, Medusa was a mortal. Being of human flesh and blood Medusa was at a bit of a disadvantage, although having the ability to turn men to stone with a glace was a plus point. Her head was finally removed from her body by Perseus, he used a reflective shield, winged boots, a large sword and the ability to become invisible to achieve it. Once her head was chopped off, the winged horse Pegasus and the giant Khrysaor emerged from the wound. Call upon the Gorgons for wisdom, knowledge, strength, power, vulnerability, rebirth, transformation, intuition, dreams, insight, clarity, past lives.

Tlazolteotl – an Aztec and Toltec goddess of guilty pleasures (think we are gonna like this one). Her name translates as 'earth, filth or dirt goddess'. She not only encourages carnal acts but then forgives them afterwards. She takes the sins of her worshippers and absorbs them into herself. As an ancient Aztec if you had an affair (and were found out) the penalty was death. However, if you professed your sin to the goddess Tlazolteotl she would forgive you and the penalty of death would be lifted. However, you only got one confession per lifetime, so you had to be careful. She had four different manifestations; a young carefree temptress, a destructive goddess of gambling, a goddess able to absorb sin and then a horrific hag who preys on the young.

Call upon Tlazolteotl for forgiveness, fertility, sexuality, moon magic, death and rebirth.

Matriarch correspondences
Moon phase: Waning
Season: Autumn
Direction: West
Element: Water

Herbs, plants and foods
Trust your intuition when choosing what ingredients to work with for this phase of the Goddess. However, here are my suggestions based on the qualities this facet of the Goddess brings:

African violet, alyssum, baking powder, banana, bay, benzoin, black pepper, beech, beef, bergamot (orange), butter, camellia, cheese, chestnut, chillies, chrysanthemum, cinnamon, clover, cucumber, crab, cumin, dates, dill, dragon's blood, echinacea, fennel, frankincense, game, ginger, goldenrod, grapes, heliotrope, holly, honey, ice cream, lemon balm, lily of the valley, liver, lobster, mango, milk, mustard, oak, olives, orchid, peach, plum, rose, rowan, sage, self-heal, Solomon's seal, soya, star anise, strawberry, sunflower, sweet pea, vanilla, wine, yew, yogurt.

Crystals
Again, go with your intuition on this and what you have available. A small tumble stone crystal is just as magical as a large, more expensive piece. And natural items all have magic within, if all you have to hand is a pebble or a shell then that will work perfectly. However, if you like to work with crystals, here are my suggestions to correspond with this phase of the Goddess:

Agate, blue lace agate, moss agate, amber, amethyst, bloodstone, calcite (orange), carnelian, celestite, chrysocolla, chrysoprase, citrine, copper, fluorite, garnet, gold, goldstone, jasper (grey), jade (nephrite), kyanite, labradorite, lapis lazuli, larimar, lepidolite, malachite, moonstone, obsidian (black), petrified wood, pyrite, quartz, quartz (rose), rhodochrosite, rhodonite, selenite, serpentine, silver, sodalite, sugilite, sunstone, tiger's eye, tourmaline, turquoise, unakite.

Modern Meet the Matriarch Meditation

I have given a meditation here that shows the matriarch in a more modern situation. Make yourself comfortable in a space where you won't be disturbed. Close your eyes and focus on your breathing, deep breaths in and deep breaths out.

As your world around you dissipates you find yourself standing on a train station platform. It seems to be early in the morning and the station is quiet with only one or two people standing further along the platform.

Then you hear the noise of a train as it enters the station, carriages going past you until it comes to a complete stop. In front of you double doors on the train open with a swish.

You step into the train and are met by a conductor who asks to see your ticket. You pat your pockets and find a train ticket in one of them and hand it over. The conductor clips it and directs you to the first-class carriage.

You head through and find your seat and sit down on plush seats behind a central table.

In front of you is an older person who is immaculately dressed, absolute head to foot elegance.

With a large briefcase beside them, they are shuffling piles of paper on the table and writing notes in a leather-bound notebook.

Looking up as you sit down, they apologise for the mess and taking up so much of the table with their paperwork. You wave your hand

and tell them not to worry.

As you make yourself comfortable the train begins to pull out of the station.

The person clears away the paperwork and looks up at you and smiles. Apologising again but explaining they are on the way to the city to give their first ever lecture at the main museum. They are excited but nervous as well.

You begin a conversation; they tell you that after retiring they took up a hobby in a field they had always loved and ended up being hired as a lecturer on the subject.

Talking about their career and now new life path they ask you questions too, encouraging you to follow your dreams and goals and to make time for yourself.

The chat is fascinating, and they are clearly very dedicated and enthusiastic about their new pathway.

Listen to what they have to say...

Then the train begins to slow as it pulls into the next station, the final destination for your companion. They thank you for listening as they gather up all their belongings. And you thank them for their time and advice.

Once the train has stopped you both head for the doors and step out of the train onto the platform. They wave as they head off.

Remember what you talked about.

When you are ready slowly and gently come back to this reality. Wriggle your fingers and toes and open your eyes. Have something to eat and drink.

A Ritual of Self Confidence

The matriarch energy is totally kick butt. Fierce, strong and standing in your own power. This stage is all about having achieved what you want in life, or at least a fair way towards it and living the life you want. It is all about strength and self-confidence. Take on that energy and follow your heart, you should be doing exactly your own thing and to Hades with anyone that thinks otherwise. Use the matriarch energy to give yourself a self confidence boost, she won't stand any nonsense. Go get 'em!

You will need:
Candles and safe holders or symbols for each quarter if using
Lighter
Incense (optional)
Something comfortable to sit or lie on
A drum or meditation music (optional)
A crystal for self-confidence, I would suggest carnelian, goldstone, labradorite or pyrite, but go with what you have, what you are drawn to or pick one from the suggested matriarch crystal list in this book.

Cast your circle by walking deosil (clockwise), if you are limited for space, stand and turn around on the spot. Visualise a circle of light surrounding you and then going above and below to form a sphere. If you have the room, you could sprinkle dried herbs or flowers to create the circle. If you are outside, please don't use anything that is not biodegradable. Say:
Goddess power to create a round
With matriarch energy this circle is bound

Call in the quarters. This can be done completely with visualisation, but you can also light a candle for each direction. As you call each quarter see and feel the qualities of that element. Or you could place items at each compass point, such as a bowl of salt for north/earth, incense for east/air, a candle for south/fire and a bowl of water for west/water.

Turn to the East and say:
Element of air with your intellect and wisdom I invite you to join

my rite today. Welcome!

Turn to the South and say:
> *Element of fire with your passion and creativity I invite you to join my rite today. Welcome!*

Turn to the West and say:
> *Element of water with your intuition and emotions I invite you to join my rite today. Welcome!*

Turn to the North and say:
> *Element of earth with your grounding and stability I invite you to join my rite today. Welcome!*

Call in the matriarch. I have chosen Lilith for this ritual but be guided by whichever goddess you feel will work for you.

> *I call upon the strong and powerful goddess Lilith, in your guise as matriarch.*
> *And ask that you join me today and lend your energies of confidence, courage and independence to my rite.*
> *Welcome!*

Light some incense if you wish and drum or put on some soft music. Sit or lie down comfortably. Take your chosen crystal and hold it in your hand. Feel a connection to the energy of the crystal. Close your eyes and focus on your breathing, deep breaths in and deep breaths out.

> *As your world around you dissipates you find yourself standing on top of a cliff, the sky above you is clear, the sun is shining and the soil beneath your feet is dry and dusty.*
> *Birds are circling high above you and you hear their calls.*
> *Take a look around you, the landscape is quite barren, but you see*

another hilltop some distance away, separated from you by a deep chasm.

You spot something near the edge of the cliff top and realise it might be a bridge, so you make your way towards it.

Indeed, it is a bridge, a narrow wooden bridge suspended by thick rope that strings its way from the edge you are standing on across the chasm to the other side.

Then you realise walking across the bridge is a figure, heading towards you. They stride across the bridge with confidence, standing tall and fearless.

It is a woman dressed in animal skins and furs, with the air of a warrior about her.

She alights from the bridge and stands in front of you and tips her head slightly in welcome.

This is the goddess Lilith. You are a little in awe of her.

She takes your hand and turns, gesturing for you to follow her back over the bridge.

You are hesitant, the bridge is long and narrow and high above the chasm. She turns back to you and asks:

"What do you fear in life?"

"What do you fear about yourself?"

"What do you fear about your abilities?"

You find yourself answering her questions truly and honestly.

Take your time, she listens and answers in detail, pay heed to her words.

When you are ready, she takes your hand again and leads you to the bridge, you feel confident enough with her support and guidance to step on to the wooden slats of the bridge.

Slowly and carefully you take more steps, Lilith leads you and guides you every step of the way.

Halfway across she stops and hands you a pebble. She tells you to put all your fears into the stone, let the fearful energy leave you and enter the pebble.

Once you are done, she instructs you to throw the pebble over the side of the bridge and you watch it fall downwards, let go of your fears as it falls.

She smiles at you and continues to cross the bridge; you follow her again but this time without her help.

Once you reach the other side, she hugs you, then steps back and hands you a gift.

You thank her for her help, and she reminds you that she is always there if you need her help again.

Turning on the spot a huge pair of wings unfurl from her shoulders and she takes flight. You watch as she heads off up into the sky.

Open your hand and see what gift she gave you. What is it? What does it mean to you?

Think about what you have seen and heard and the meaning behind the gift you were given.

Slowly and gently come back to this reality, wriggle your fingers and toes and open your eyes. Eat and drink something. If you are outside don't forget to share some of your drink or food to the earth as a blessing.

Thank Lilith:

I give my thanks to the strong and powerful goddess Lilith, in your guise as matriarch

For joining me today and lending your energies of confidence, courage and independence to my rite. Go if you must but stay if you will. With my gratitude and thanks, farewell.

Thank the quarters:

Turn to the North and say:

Element of earth with your grounding and stability I thank you for joining my rite today. Farewell!

Turn to the West and say:

Element of water with your intuition and emotions I thank you for joining my rite today. Farewell!

Turn to the South and say:
*Element of fire with your passion and creativity I thank you for
joining my rite today. Farewell!*

Turn to the East and say:
*Element of air with your intellect and wisdom I thank you for
joining my rite today. Farewell!*

Close the circle by walking widdershins (anti-clockwise) around
your circle or turn around on the spot. Visualise the sphere
dissipating and the circle disappearing. Say:
Goddess power dissolve this circle round
With thanks for the matriarch energy this circle is unwound

The Crone

Onto the crone phase, she is the wise woman and the sage.
Our ancestors would have revered the crone for her wisdom,
knowledge and possibly the actual fact that she survived to old
age. Sadly, I think the pensioners of our modern age don't always
get revered or even respected which is a real shame because they
have so much knowledge and insight to share. Although as time
moves on the pensioners now are possibly more likely to be
riding Harleys and taking holidays to the South of France rather
than retiring to the seaside to sit in a deckchair and eat fish and
chips.

The word 'crone' comes from the Greek word 'cronos' which
means 'time'. Interestingly the name for the Hindu goddess Kali
derives from the Sanskrit 'kale' which also means 'time'.

The crone is the Winter phase of life, wisdom, knowledge,
experience, guidance and transformation in the guise of
destruction and death which brings the circle around again to
new life and new beginnings. The archetypical image of a crone,

is that of an old woman with white hair, a hunched figure and a wrinkled face. A huge percentage of our pensioner generation today won't fit that image at all. Most will still be fighting the battle of hiding the grey hair under hair dye (I started that mission a long time ago), be dressed fashionably and still be rocking the 'live life to the fullest' idea. But it is the phase in your life journey that maybe gives you the most time to yourself, retirement offers days free to follow pursuits, jet off around the world or just to potter about in the garden, reading, relaxing and perhaps spending time with your grandchildren. Not so relaxing if you are grandparents though, because our generation relies a huge amount on grandparents looking after the grandchildren so that the parents can still go to work. My parents, who have been retired and grandparents for quite a number of years now are well dressed, love going out to dinner and take lots of holidays. No deckchair on the beach for them!

There are many crone goddesses such as the Cailleach (my own personal matron Goddess), Kali and Macha. A lot of the crone goddesses are also linked with death and destruction and to me that makes sense. There may come time in your life when you think "I must have less years left in my lifetime than those I have already lived" and that can be pretty scary. I believe that part of the crone phase in your life is to accept that life is a cycle, a never ending one, one of birth, life, death and rebirth. Thinking about death is not pleasant but it is a reality and one that should hopefully make us think about how we are as a person, what kind of life we live and how we have treated others. The crone stage is also one of introspection and maybe even one of making amends. Do you get to the crone stage and think about all the decisions you have made, all the people you have helped…or not helped, those that you have hurt or cared for? It is an interesting exercise to do when you are in your twenties, thirties or forties but I would imagine extremely eye opening to look back over say eighty years and review every part of your journey, good or bad.

The question is...when you get to the crone stage what will you think and feel when you look back over your lifetime?

Alternative name suggestions:
- Winter
- North
- Earth
- Dark
- Midnight
- Caves
- Wisdom
- Wise
- Elder
- Wise One
- Protector
- Knowledge
- Mature
- Act Four
- Light
- Independent
- Grandmother
- Beldam
- Oldster
- Golden ager
- Senior
- Veteran
- Cunning Woman
- Sovereign

The Crone Attributes:
- Balance
- Comfort
- Culmination
- Death

- Destruction
- Divination
- End of cycles
- Endings
- Experience
- Fulfilment
- Guidance
- Harvest
- Justice
- Knowledge
- Meditation
- Mysteries
- Past Lives
- Prophecy
- Protection
- Rebirth
- Relaxation
- Retribution
- Spirit World Connection
- Support
- Transformation
- Truth
- Understanding
- Visions
- Winter
- Wisdom

Crone Goddesses

Annis – The stories of Black Annis seem to be centred in and around the area of Leicester in England, but all suggest that she is a hag, a bringer of death and the winter. In all the tales she is described as being extremely tall with blue skin and usually with talons and/or long teeth and one eye and generally favours the bad habit of eating people, particularly children, and was often blamed for the death or disappearance of livestock. She would wait in her cave ready to pounce on any children that wandered too far from the village. Once she devoured the children, she would hang their skins out to dry. Perhaps this was a bit of an embellishment on the story to stop children from misbehaving.

I do think maybe she was the goddess that looked after the souls of those children that passed away too young. And perhaps also as the culler for herds of animals, taking the lives of those that were weak allowing the strongest to survive. I also believe that she has a strong connection with The Cailleach. Call upon Black Annis for balance, rebirth, cycles, overcoming hardship, honesty, winter, night, nature.

Badb – an Irish goddess known as one of the Morrigans. Her name translates as hooded crow or deadly. She is a shapeshifter, turning into a crow. A lot of her stories surround battles of one kind or another. She is said to turn into a crow and fly across battlefields screeching to cause chaos and panic. Call upon Badb for divination, warrior energy, battle, magic, wisdom, shape shifting.

Baba Yaga – a Slovenian goddess of death and rebirth. Stories describe her as an old hag who lives in a house made from animal bones that stands on chicken leg supports surrounded with a fence made from human bones and skulls. Others suggest that she sometimes appears as a young woman. The name Baba translates as grandmother. She represents the cycle of death and rebirth and has a strong connection to the harvest. Call upon Baba Yaga for cycles, death and rebirth, wisdom, harvest, gratitude, renewal, truth.

Hekate – A goddess of magic, Witchcraft and the crossroads, she hails from Greece. Hekate guided the goddess Demeter with flaming torches when looking for her daughter Persephone. The name Hekate translates as 'worker from afar'. She has many titles such as Dark Queen, Dark Mother and Dark Maiden. Often viewed as an individual deity, she also has a triple form. She can be seen in the form of a young nymph or a crone. In her triple form her image is that of one body with three animal heads. Her many guises reflect the different stages of life. Although she is seen as both a younger woman and a crone, I have put her here because I believe her attributes align more with those of the crone phase. Call upon Hekate for prosperity, decisions, direction, protection, inner work, moon magic, beginnings, magic of all kinds, opportunity.

Cerridwen – a Welsh goddess of inspiration and transformation. Her cauldron is filled with the Awen, the spirit of inspiration. She brewed a potion to transform her ugly son, but it took a year and a day to create. During that time a boy, Gwion Bach tended to the fire below the cauldron. He upset the cauldron and a few drops fell upon him, transforming him into a great magician. Cerridwen ran after him and the following chase was something from a comedy sketch with them shape shifting into various forms until he changed into a kernel of grain and she, as a hen pecked him up. Nine months later she gave birth to Taliesin who became a bard, probably the greatest. Call upon Cerridwen for creativity, inspiration, wisdom, good luck, harvest, fertility, transformation, death and rebirth, renewal.

Cailleach (The) – Ancient British goddess of the ancestors, wisdom that comes with age, the weather, time, shape shifting and winter. She is said to have shaped the landscape by dropping boulders from her apron which given that she is often portrayed as a giant should have been a fairly easy task. Her time is Samhain to Beltane which is when she is at her most powerful. And powerful she most certainly is for in my experience she is a strong, feisty, no nonsense, and kick bottom goddess with a wicked sense of humour. Often referred to as a Neolithic goddess her origins seem to lie in ancient Britain but traces of her can be found across Europe, still as part of Celtic tribal history but in places such as Greece, Spain and Portugal. Call upon the Cailleach for balance, rebirth, cycles, overcoming hardship, honesty, winter, night, nature, shape shifting, weather magic, wisdom.

Fates, The – Here we have the Greek goddesses of fate. The name 'fates' translates as 'parts, shares or portions'. The threads of life are spun by Klotho (Clotho) who carries a spindle. The 'apportioner of lots' measuring out fate is Lakhesis (Lachesis) who carries a staff. And 'she who cannot be turned' cutting it down short is Atropos (Asia) who carries a scroll or scales. The team was led by the god of fate, Zeus Moiragetes. The Fates are responsible for weaving the thread of fate when a human is born. It isn't a set future though, if Zeus wants to change the course of any fate he will step in and divert it. Humans themselves do have a hand in their own destiny though. This set of ladies are extremely powerful and can set or change the course of fate for any human. Not blessed in the looks department, the Fates are said to be old, ugly women. Call upon The Fates for, well fate really! Divination, destiny and finding a direction.

Kali Ma – Kali is the Hindu destroyer goddess, fearsome and keeper of time, she is also a creator. Seen with blue or black skin and wearing skulls around her neck. Her name translates as 'the Black Goddess'. You cannot have rebirth without death, she brings both. Kali fought the lord of demons, but every time a drop of his blood touched the earth a thousand more demons emerged. Her solution was to lick up every drop of blood, bringing her success in the battle. The problem was, she was so delirious with success that she danced, and danced bringing more destruction. The gods tried to stop her, but she was not listening and when her husband, the god Shiva tried, she didn't recognize him and threw him to the ground dancing over him. Call upon Kali Ma for death and rebirth, cycles, courage, hope, change, transformation, cleansing, time, happiness.

Manat – one of the triad of goddesses from pre-Islamic Arabia. Manat means fate, time or destruction, she is often depicted as the crone. She has connection to a sanctuary that was the point where people set off on pilgrimages. Worship of her is very ancient and seems to be focused at Quidaid near Mecca. Her sanctuary is the starting point for many pilgrimages. She is a goddess of death and would protect tombs from those wishing to desecrate them. Call upon Manat for protection, fate, waning moon magic.

Mórrígan – an Irish goddess. The name translates as Nightmare/Phantom Queen or Great Queen. Her sisters are Macha and Badb along with Eriu, Fotla and Banba. Another deity that graces the battlefields (along with her sisters). She is a powerful sorceress who is a well-practiced shape shifter often appearing as a crow or a raven. She can also be seen as a beautiful young woman or and old crone. Call upon the Morrigan for magic, victory, success, divination, warrior energy

Frau Holle/Holda – has a very ancient Germanic history perhaps even dating back to Neolithic times. She began as a goddess of death and rebirth tying her into the cycles of life and the seasons of the earth. As a goddess of death, she is associated with winter. She brings the storms, protects children and works with all the crafts and domestic arts such as spinning. She does not tolerate laziness in any form. Holda brings the first snow of the year, by shaking her goose filled pillows out of the windows. You will also find reference to her as a goddess of the Underworld. Call upon Holle/Holda for wisdom, magic, destiny, karma, protection, the home, productivity, longevity, insight.

Nicneven – a Scottish crone goddess. She is a goddess with connections to the Otherworld and the festival of Samhain. Nicneven is said to be a Queen of the Faerie world. Call upon Nicneven for protection, divination, peace, magic, winter, Otherworld connection, wisdom.

Nephthys – one of the original five gods of ancient Egypt, her parents are the earth and the sky. Her name translates as 'lady of the temple', which is basically 'woman who rules the house'. So, you don't want to forget to wipe your feet when you come in. She protects the souls of her people and as such is associated with death and rebirth. Originally, she was invoked during funeral services. Call upon Nephthys for death and rebirth, devotion, protection, Otherworld connection.

Sekhmet – one of the most ancient Egyptian goddesses, seen with a lion head. The name Sekhmet translates as 'powerful one'. Perhaps an opposite to the fun and happy goddess Hathor, Sekhmet is the darker aspect. Amenemhet II dedicated a temple to both Hathor and Sekhmet. Sometimes known as 'the destroyer' she is the power of the sun at its height and was seen by her followers as mighty and powerful. Perhaps even a little scary. Although she brings life and healing, she has the power to destroy and create. And if you upset her? Be prepared for a plague to come your way. Call upon Sekhmet death and rebirth, healing, control of your temper, change, releasing, forgiveness.

Sedna – an Inuit goddess of the sea and the animals within the waters. Offerings are made to her for protection against her wrath and for good hunting. She lives under the waves in a house made from whale bones and stones. All sea creatures are said to have been created from her. Call upon Sedna for power, buried emotions, depression, releasing, abundance, nature, gratitude.

Crone correspondences
Moon phase: Dark
Season: Winter
Direction: North
Element: Earth

Herbs, plants and foods

Trust your intuition when choosing what ingredients to work with for this phase of the Goddess. However, here are my suggestions based on the qualities this facet of the Goddess brings:

Almond, aloe, angelica, apple, bay, bean, beech, belladonna, blackthorn, bladder wrack, bluebell, borage, buttercup, cherry, chicken, cinquefoil, cinnamon, clove, coffee, cornflower (batchelor's buttons), cramp bark, dandelion, dates, echinacea, eggs, elder, elm, eucalyptus, fenugreek, fern, figs, foxglove, game, grass, hazel, honeysuckle, honesty, iris, juniper, lemongrass, lily of the valley, mace, marigold, morning glory, mugwort, mustard, myrrh, pansy, pasta, pine, pistachio, plum, pomegranate, poppy, rose, rowan, saffron, sage, Saint John's Wort, sandalwood (white), snapdragon, Solomon's seal, soya, star anise, sunflower, sweet pea, tansy, thyme, violet, wheat, witch hazel, wormwood, yew.

Crystal

Again, go with your intuition on this and what you have available. A small tumble stone crystal is just as magical as a large, more expensive piece. And natural items all have magic within, if all you have to hand is a pebble or a shell then that will work perfectly. However, if you like to work with crystals, here are my suggestions to correspond with this phase of the

Goddess:

Agate, agate (blue lace), agate (moss), amber, amethyst, aventurine (green), bloodstone, carnelian, chrysoprase, chrysocolla, citrine, copper, fluorite, garnet, gold, goldstone, hematite, Howlite, jade (nephrite), jasper (red), kyanite, labradorite, lapis lazuli, larimar, lepidolite, malachite, moonstone, obsidian (black), petrified wood, pyrite, quartz, quartz (smoky), rhodochrosite, rhodonite, selenite, silver, sodalite, sugilite, tiger's eye, tourmaline, turquoise, unakite.

Modern Meet the Crone Meditation

I have given a meditation here that shows the crone in a more modern situation. Make yourself comfortable in a space where you won't be disturbed. Close your eyes and focus on your breathing, deep breaths in and deep breaths out.

As your world around you dissipates you find yourself standing outside a large industrial looking wooden door in the side of a warehouse.

It slides open as you are standing there. You are greeted by an elderly but spritely person, dressed in a flowy multi coloured kaftan, with wild silver white hair and seemingly a long paint brush poked behind their ear. Looking down you notice that on their feet are sparkly purple Doc Marten books.

When they see you standing there they smile and throw their arms in the air. Exclaiming a loud and enthusiastic welcome to you. You are ushered inside.

Which opens up to the inside of the warehouse, the walls all pristine white and the floors a pale bleached wood.

And all around the walls are huge floor to ceiling canvas images, beautiful, haunting and striking artwork.

The person brings you over a tall glass of cold drink and offers it to you.

98

Then asks why you are here, to which you answer that you are not sure.

The reply is to offer to show you around, which you accept.

They begin by explaining that they are the artist and although they have loved to paint all their life, they have only recently had the time and the money to do so properly. This is their first gallery exhibition. The images tell the story of their life so far.

Leading you to the first painting you are asked to look at it and tell them what you see.

Take your time and study the image, what do you see, what feelings does it inspire?

Talk to them about it and get their perspective too.

Walk around the whole exhibition, they lead you to each painting in turn and you both discuss your feelings about each one.

Once you have seen it all you are invited to sit on a large comfortable couch with them and talk about what you have seen and felt.

Take your time and listen to what they have to tell you.

When you are ready you thank them for their time and guidance, and they lead you back to the door. Waving you goodbye as you step outside.

Remember what you have talked about.

When you are ready slowly and gently come back to this reality. Wriggle your fingers and toes and open your eyes. Have something to eat and drink.

A Ritual of Transformation

The crone energy is one of wisdom but also for changes and transformation. She has pretty much seen everything, done everything and got the t-shirt, this gal knows her stuff. The crone also knows that destruction must occur before renewal and transformation can happen. You gotta tear down the old that you are hanging on to, for the changes and life changing regeneration to happen. Don't hang onto things that no longer serve you, don't hang on to old bad habits and toxic cycles, they just fester. Do something about it now...

You will need:

Candles and safe holders or symbols for each quarter if using
Lighter
Incense (optional)
Something comfortable to sit or lie on
A drum or meditation music (optional)
A crystal for transformation, I would suggest amethyst, red jasper, malachite or petrified wood, but go with what you have, what you are drawn to or pick one from the suggested crone crystal list in this book.

Cast your circle by walking deosil (clockwise), if you are limited for space, stand and turn around on the spot. Visualise a circle of light surrounding you and then going above and below to form a sphere. If you have the room, you could sprinkle dried herbs or flowers to create the circle. If you are outside, please don't use anything that is not biodegradable. Say:

Goddess power to create a round
With crone energy this circle is bound

Call in the quarters. This can be done completely with visualisation, but you can also light a candle for each direction. As you call each quarter see and feel the qualities of that element. Or you could place items at each compass point, such as a bowl of salt for north/earth, incense for east/air, a candle for south/fire and a bowl of water for west/water.

Turn to the East and say:

Element of air with your intellect and wisdom I invite you to join my rite today. Welcome!

Turn to the South and say:

Element of fire with your passion and creativity I invite you to join my rite today. Welcome!

Turn to the West and say:

Element of water with your intuition and emotions I invite you to join my rite today. Welcome!

Turn to the North and say:

Element of earth with your grounding and stability I invite you to join my rite today. Welcome!

Call in the crone. I have chosen Baba Yaga for this ritual but be guided by whichever goddess you feel will work for you.

I call upon the wise goddess Baba Yaga, in your guise as crone. And ask that you join me today and lend your energies of transformation and renewal to my rite. Welcome!

Light some incense if you wish and drum or put on some soft music. Sit or lie down comfortably. Take your chosen crystal and hold it in your hand. Feel a connection to the energy of the crystal. Close your eyes and focus on your breathing, deep breaths in and deep breaths out.

As your world around you dissipates you find yourself standing deep in a swamp like forest. Canopies of dark green foliage from trees arch over your head, with tendrils of plants hanging down from the branches.

There is a wide river slowly making its way past, the waters are deep and dark.

You can hear animal and bird noises from further in the forest.

You hear a sound from the water and a small wooden boat is pulling up to the water's edge, there is no one in it and the boat seems to be guiding itself.

You are drawn to investigate so you head over and find yourself stepping down into the boat. As you do a lantern in the front lights up with the flickering flame of a big fat white candle set inside it.

You sit down and the boat begins to slowly move, heading down the river.

Take a look around you at your surroundings, at the trees and creepers, the animals on the riverbank and high in the branches above you.

The boat starts to veer towards one side of the riverbank, and you notice a strange looking house on the side. A small wooden shack is lifted up off the ground and supported by what appears to be chicken legs.

As you draw closer you can see the shack is not made from wood as you first thought, but an intricate design created from bones of all shapes and sizes.

Large lanterns are strung outside, each one similar to the one in your boat. Wind chimes made from seed pods and shells are strung across the porch.

The boat stops right outside, and you step out onto the land. Heading upwards to the strange house and climbing the steps to the front door.

As you arrive, the door swings open and you step inside.

The air is warm and smells of spices and herbs. It too is filled with the candle lanterns which throw a warm light around the room. The walls are covered with shelves, each one packed with row upon row of jars filled with unidentifiable herbs and spices...and other things.

A voice makes you jump "sit down"

As your eyes adjust to the candlelight you realise there is an old woman sitting in a large rocking chair in the corner. She looks at you and gestures for you to sit beside her.

She asks you why you are here.

Then she asks, "What do you wish to release?"

"What do you want to change about yourself?"

"What do you want to change about your life?"

You find yourself answering her honestly. She listens and replies, reminding you that you must first let go and clear out before any changes can be made. And that you are the one that can make those changes.

She also tells you that you have made the first step by following the river to her.

She hands you a bowl full of shells, instructing you to take them back in the boat with you.

You thank her and she ushers you out of the door, where the boat is waiting for you.

Climbing into the boat again you sit down with the bowl of shells on your lap.

Once the boat starts moving you feel a sudden urge to throw one of the shells into the water, with it you say out loud something that you want to release or get rid of.

Keep doing this with as many shells as you need.

When you are done you find the boat has arrived back where you started so you climb out, realizing that you have one shell left, so you pick it up and hold on to it. This is a reminder of your transformation journey.

Think about what you have seen and heard and prepare yourself for your transformation to begin.

Slowly and gently come back to this reality, wriggle your fingers and toes and open your eyes. Eat and drink something. If you are outside don't forget to share some of your drink or food to the earth as a blessing.

Thank Baba Yaga:

I give my thanks to the wise goddess Baba Yaga, in your guise as crone

For joining me today and lending your energies of transformation and renewal to my rite. Go if you must but stay if you will. With my gratitude and thanks, farewell.

Thank the quarters:
Turn to the North and say:
Element of earth with your grounding and stability I thank you for joining my rite today. Farewell!

Turn to the West and say:
Element of water with your intuition and emotions I thank you for joining my rite today. Farewell!

Turn to the South and say:
Element of fire with your passion and creativity I thank you for joining my rite today. Farewell!

Turn to the East and say:
Element of air with your intellect and wisdom I thank you for joining my rite today. Farewell!

Close the circle by walking widdershins (anti-clockwise) around your circle or turn around on the spot. Visualise the sphere dissipating and the circle disappearing. Say:
Goddess power dissolve this circle round
With thanks for the crone energy this circle is unwound

Goddesses through the Seasons

I often work with the energy of the season or even the month or week. This works well tying in with deity too. How about working with a different goddess for each season or even each month? You could work with the same goddess for three months at a time or a different one each month.

Spring – March, April, May – work with maiden goddesses

Summer – June, July, August – work with mother goddesses
Autumn – September, October, November – work with matriarch goddesses
Winter – November, December, January – work with crone goddesses

Meeting the Goddesses Meditation

This meditation takes more of a traditional view of the Goddesses. Find a space where you won't be disturbed and make yourself comfortable. Close your eyes and focus on your breathing. Deep breaths in...deep breaths out...

As the world around you dissipates you find yourself standing in front of a large ornate wooden door set into a grand stone building. You push the door and it swings open with a loud creak.

Step inside.

The door opens to reveal a huge circular stone hallway. Polished stone on the floor underfoot and marble walls and ceilings.

In the centre stands large brass compass, ornately decorated with jewels and precious stones. The compass shows all four directions – north, east, south and west.

Make your way to foot of the compass and take a look around you.

There are four more doorways leading from the hallway, one behind you, next to the entrance. One to the left, one to the right and a fourth one in front of you.

Take a walk around and look at each doorway starting with the one to your left, the one shown on the compass as 'west'.

The archway to the door is decorated with shells and sea glass. When you step closer to the doorway you can just hear the sound of the ocean.

Walk onto the next doorway.

This one has an archway covered with sparkling quartz crystals and as you step closer you can hear the faint beat of a drum; the compass shows this one to be 'north'.

Onwards around to the third doorway, the archway to this one is covered with all kinds of spring flowers in white and yellow. The compass points to this doorway as 'east'. As you step closer the faint sounds of a harp playing beautiful music reach your ears.

And on to the fourth doorway, this one has an archway created from red and orange glass tiles, set in a mosaic pattern. Marked by the compass, this one is 'south'. As you step closer a scent catches your nose, the deep musky smell of frankincense wafts past you.

You turn and head back to the centre and sit on the edge of the fountain.

Four doorways, each one leading you to a different experience. Which one are you drawn to?

You can start with one and work your way around to each in turn. You may just be drawn to one in particular.

Make your choice...

If you chose the doorway to the east, head to the archway covered with spring flowers.

Step through the entrance.

The air is full with the scent of spring flowers and you can hear bees buzzing and birds singing. Above that you can also hear the sound of a harp being played beautifully.

A few steps in and the world opens up around you, to a field full of tall grasses and wildflowers.

Take a look around at the scenery, breathe deeply, listen and take notice.

Follow the sound of the harp, it leads you through the field with grasses and flowers either side of you, bees buzzing around you and birds flying above.

In the centre of the field is a small clearing and there you find the person playing the harp.

They beckon you forward and invite you to sit down.

Making yourself comfortable you close your eyes and listen to the sounds of the harp, letting them wash over you.

Finally, the person speaks; telling you they are the embodiment of spring, of youth and innocence.

They may share a message with you, please do ask questions of them, pay attention to the answers.

They also encourage you to look within, to seek your inner child and to carry the attributes of spring back into the world with you.

When you are ready, thank them and stand up.

Make your way back across the field to the entrance where you came in.

Step out through the doorway and back into the central hallway.

If you chose the doorway to the south, head to the archway covered with glass mosaic.

Step through the entrance.

The air is heavy with incense, strong heady frankincense and myrrh. But it isn't overwhelming, and you find you can breathe easily.

A few steps in and the world opens up around you, to a forest full of dark green trees their canopies stretching high above you, the sunlight just peeping through. With a floor full of moss and ferns beneath your feet.

Follow the scent and smoke from the incense as it leads you along a small pathway through the trees.

Listen to the sounds around you and take note of anything that you see.

The pathway opens to reveal a small clearing, in the centre is a large stone lying flat on its side. A round dish laying on top of the stone appears to be the source of the incense, smoke snakes up from inside and disperses into the air. There is a person standing behind it, taking pinches of ingredients and sprinkling them onto the charcoal.

They beckon you forward and invite you to sit down beside the stone.

Making yourself comfortable you close your eyes and allow the scent of the incense to flow over you.

Finally, the person speaks, telling you they are the embodiment of summer, of nurturing and maturity.

They may share a message with you, please do ask questions of them, pay attention to the answers.

They also encourage you to look within, to seek time for self-care and respect and to carry the attributes of summer back into the world with you.

When you are ready, thank them and stand back up.

Make your way back through the trees to the entrance where you came in.

Step out through the doorway and back into the central hallway.

If you chose the doorway to the west, head to the archway covered with shells and sea glass.

Step through the entrance.

You can hear the sound of the ocean in the distance and smell the salty sea air.

A few steps in and the world opens up around you, to a seashore, the ocean waves in front of you and sand beneath your feet. Seagulls circle overhead, shouting loudly on the breeze.

You walk over the sand and head to the shoreline, where the waves are gently lapping the beach.

As you stand looking out across the water someone walks towards you, looking up at them, they invite you to sit on the sand with them.

They begin to create patterns in the sand with pebbles and shells, you sit and watch.

Finally, the person speaks, telling you they are the embodiment of autumn, of confidence and transformation.

They may share a message with you, please do ask questions of them, pay attention to the answers.

They also encourage you to seek your inner courage and stand proud and to carry the attributes of autumn back into the world with you.

When you are ready, thank them and stand back up.

Make your way back across the sand to the entrance where you came in.

Step out through the doorway and back into the central hallway.

If you chose the doorway to the north, head to the archway covered with quartz crystals.

Step through the entrance.

You can hear the sound of a drum beating slowly and gently.

A few steps in and the world opens up around you, to a cave where the walls around you, the floor beneath you and the ceiling above you are made entirely from crystals. All different sizes, shapes and colours, some rough, some smooth.

It is dark, give your eyes a moment to adjust to the lanterns hung from the walls.

In the centre of the cave is a pile of blankets and cushions, laid out like a bed. Standing beside it is a person, beating a drum.

You listen for a moment, they beckon to you to come forward and lay down, to make yourself comfortable on the blankets.

Close your eyes and allow the sound of the drum to flow through you.

Finally, the person speaks, telling you they are the embodiment of winter, of wisdom and experience.

They may share a message with you, please do ask questions of them, pay attention to the answers. They also encourage you to seek your inner knowledge and to trust your intuition.

When you are ready, thank them and stand up.

Make your way back across the cave to the entrance where you came in.

Step out through the doorway and back into the central hallway.

Once you have finished visiting one, some or all of the directions.

Turn to face the compass.
Understand that there are many pathways and directions you can
take; the choice is yours. Know that you can return to this place any
time you feel the need. When you are ready head back towards the
entrance where you came in, stepping out through the large wooden
door and back into reality.

Slowly and gently come back, wriggle your fingers and toes and open your eyes. Have a drink and something to eat. Write down any important information.

A Goddess ending

Whatever way you work with the Goddesses, in whichever phase they are, or you are, they are there to help, support and guide you. All you need to do is ask. Well actually that's not technically true is it? Because once you have asked, they will give you support and guidance but ultimately it is you that needs to do the real work. But it will be absolutely worth it.

Suggested Reading/Sources

Moonchild by Aleister Crowley

'The Triad of the Goddess' (an essay) by Gerald Gardner

The White Goddess by Robert Graves (although this book covers many other things as well as the Goddess)

Stalking the Goddess by Mark Carter (read The White Goddess first then this excellent book that breaks down The White Goddess)

'The Theme of the Three Caskets' (an essay) by Sigmund Freud

Triumph of the Moon by Ronald Hutton

Seneca's Medea

John Halstead's blog on Patheos Pagan has several essays about the Triple Goddess

Pagan Portals - Gods and Goddess of Ireland by Morgan Daimler

Pagan Portals - Brigid by Morgan Daimler

Pagan Portals - Hekate, a Devotional by Vivienne Moss

Pagan Portals - The Morrigan by Morgan Daimler

Pagan Portals - Hellenic Paganism by Samantha Leaver

The Legacy of Inanna by Michael Orellana

'Goddesses in Celtic Religion. Cult and Mythology: A Comparative Study of Ancient Ireland, Britain and Gaul' Doctoral Thesis by Par Noemie Beck

Bhagavad Gita, Hindu scriptures

The Cult of the Matronae in the Roman Rhineland: An Historical Evaluation of the Archaeological Evidence by Alex Garman

Pagan Goddesses in the Early Germanic World: Eostre, Hreda and the Cult of Matrons by Philip Shaw

The Mabinogion by Philip Shaw

Numerology by Elen Sentier

Journey to the Dark Goddess by Jane Meredith

Aspecting the Goddess by Jane Meredith

Naming the Goddess, a Moon Books collective, edited by Trevor Greenfield

www.theoi.com

Encyclopedia Britannica

www.ancient-literature.com

www.norse-mythology.org

https://ancientegyptonline.co.uk/

www.thaliatook.com

MOON
BOOKS

PAGANISM & SHAMANISM

What is Paganism? A religion, a spirituality, an alternative
belief system, nature worship? You can find support for
all these definitions (and many more) in dictionaries,
encyclopaedias, and text books of religion, but subscribe to
any one and the truth will evade you. Above all Paganism is
a creative pursuit, an encounter with reality, an exploration
of meaning and an expression of the soul. Druids, Heathens,
Wiccans and others, all contribute their insights and literary
riches to the Pagan tradition. Moon Books invites you to begin
or to deepen your own encounter, right here, right now.
If you have enjoyed this book, why not tell other readers by
posting a review on your preferred book site.

Recent bestsellers from Moon Books are:

Journey to the Dark Goddess
How to Return to Your Soul
Jane Meredith
Discover the powerful secrets of the Dark Goddess and
transform your depression, grief and pain into healing
and integration.
Paperback: 978-1-84694-677-6 ebook: 978-1-78099-223-5

Shamanic Reiki
Expanded Ways of Working with Universal Life Force Energy
Llyn Roberts, Robert Levy
Shamanism and Reiki are each powerful ways of healing;
together, their power multiplies. Shamanic Reiki introduces
techniques to help healers and Reiki practitioners tap ancient
healing wisdom.
Paperback: 978-1-84694-037-8 ebook: 978-1-84694-650-9

Pagan Portals – The Awen Alone
Walking the Path of the Solitary Druid
Joanna van der Hoeven
An introductory guide for the solitary Druid, The Awen Alone
will accompany you as you explore, and seek out your own
place within the natural world.
Paperback: 978-1-78279-547-6 ebook: 978-1-78279-546-9

A Kitchen Witch's World of Magical Herbs & Plants
Rachel Patterson
A journey into the magical world of herbs and plants, filled
with magical uses, folklore, history and practical magic. By
popular writer, blogger and kitchen witch, Tansy Firedragon.
Paperback: 978-1-78279-621-3 ebook: 978-1-78279-620-6

Shapeshifting into Higher Consciousness
Heal and Transform Yourself and Our World with Ancient
Shamanic and Modern Methods
Llyn Roberts
Ancient and modern methods that you can use every day to
transform yourself and make a positive difference in the world.
Paperback: 978-1-84694-843-5 ebook: 978-1-84694-844-2

Readers of ebooks can buy or view any of these bestsellers by
clicking on the live link in the title. Most titles are published
in paperback and as an ebook. Paperbacks are available in
traditional bookshops. Both print and ebook formats are
available online.

Find more titles and sign up to our readers' newsletter at
http://www.johnhuntpublishing.com/paganism
Follow us on Facebook at https://www.facebook.com/
MoonBooks
and Twitter at https://twitter.com/MoonBooksJHP

Other books by Rachel Patterson you may enjoy...

Pagan Portals - Kitchen Witchcraft

Crafts of a Kitchen Witch

978-1-78099-843-5 (Paperback)
978-1-78099-842-8 (e-book)

Pagan Portals – Moon Magic

An introduction to working with the phases of the Moon

978-1-78279-281-9 (Paperback)
978-1-78279-282-6 (e-book)

Pagan Portals – Sun Magic

How to live in harmony with the solar year

978-1-78904-101-9 (Paperback)
978-1-78904-102-6 (e-book)